THURGOOD MARSHALL

THURGOOD MARSHALL

Lisa Aldred

Senior Consulting Editor
Nathan Irvin Huggins
Director
W.E.B. Du Bois Institute for Afro-American Research
Harvard University

SCHOLASTIC INC.
Danbury, Connecticut

Editor-in-Chief Nancy Toff
Executive Editor Remmel T. Nunn
Managing Editor Karyn Gullen Browne
Copy Chief Juliann Barbato
Picture Editor Adrian G. Allen
Art Director Maria Epes
Manufacturing Manager Gerald Levine

Black Americans of Achievement
Senior Editor Richard Rennert

Staff for THURGOOD MARSHALL
Text Editor Marian Taylor
Deputy Copy Chief Mark Rifkin
Editorial Assistant Leigh Hope Wood
Picture Researcher Patricia Burns
Assistant Art Director Loraine Machlin
Designer Ghila Krajzman
Production Manager Joseph Romano
Production Coordinator Marie Claire Cebrián
Cover Illustration Daniel Mark Duffy

Published for Scholastic by Chelsea House

Frontispiece: *Thurgood Marshall, chief counsel of the National Association for the Advancement of Colored People (NAACP), confers with his staff at the NAACP's New York City headquarters.*

ISBN 0-7172 8556-1

CONTENTS

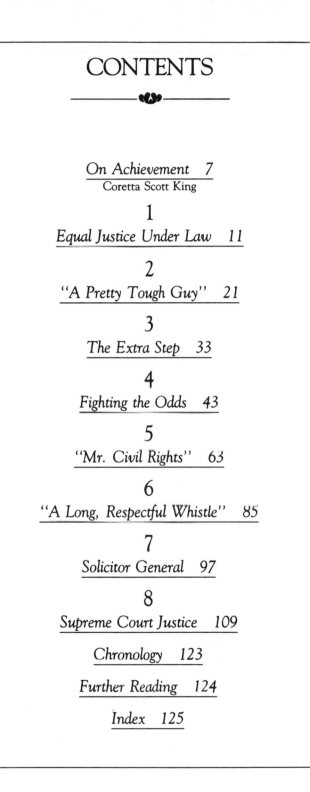

ON
ACHIEVEMENT

———— ❧ ————

Coretta Scott King

Before you begin this book, I hope you will ask yourself what the word *excellence* means to you. I think that it's a question we should all ask and keep asking as we grow older and change. Because the truest answer to it should never change. When you think of excellence, perhaps you think of success at work; or of becoming wealthy; or meeting the right person, getting married, and having a good family life.

Those important goals are worth striving for, but there is a better way to look at excellence. As Martin Luther King, Jr., said in one of his last sermons, "I want you to be first in love. I want you to be first in moral excellence. I want you to be first in generosity. If you want to be important, wonderful. If you want to be great, wonderful. But recognize that he who is greatest among you shall be your servant."

My husband, Martin Luther King, Jr., knew that the true meaning of achievement is service. When I met him, in 1952, he was already ordained as a Baptist preacher and was working toward a doctoral degree at Boston University. I was studying at the New England Conservatory and dreamed of accomplishments in music. We married a year later, and after I graduated the following year we moved to Montgomery, Alabama. We didn't know it then, but our notions of achievement were about to undergo a dramatic change.

You may have read or heard about what happened next. What began with the boycott of a local bus line grew into a national movement, and by the time he was assassinated in 1968 my husband had fashioned a black movement powerful enough to shatter forever the practice of racial segregation. What you may not have read about is where he got his method for resisting injustice without compromising his religious beliefs.

He adopted the strategy of nonviolence from a man of a different race, who lived in a distant country, and even practiced a different religion. The man was Mahatma Gandhi, the great leader of India, who devoted his life to serving humanity in the spirit of love and nonviolence. It was in these principles that Martin discovered his method for social reform. More than anything else, those two principles were the key to his achievements.

This book is about black Americans who served society through the excellence of their achievements. It forms a part of the rich history of black men and women in America—a history of stunning accomplishments in every field of human endeavor, from literature and art to science, industry, education, diplomacy, athletics, jurisprudence, even polar exploration.

Not all of the people in this history had the same ideals, but I think you will find something that all of them have in common. Like Martin Luther King, Jr., they all decided to become "drum majors" and serve humanity. In that principle—whether it was expressed in books, inventions, or song—they found something outside themselves to use as a goal and a guide. Something that showed them a way to serve others, instead of living only for themselves.

Reading the stories of these courageous men and women not only helps us discover the principles that we will use to guide our own lives but also teaches us about our black heritage and about America itself. It is crucial for us to know the heroes and heroines of our history and to realize that the price we paid in our struggle for equality in America was dear. But we must also understand that we have gotten as far as we have partly because America's democratic system and ideals made it possible.

We are still struggling with racism and prejudice. But the great men and women in this series are a tribute to the spirit of our democratic ideals and the system in which they have flourished. And that makes their stories special and worth knowing. ⚬

THURGOOD
MARSHALL

1

EQUAL JUSTICE UNDER LAW

❦

ON THE COLD morning of December 8, 1953, attorney Thurgood Marshall climbed a flight of white marble steps in Washington, D.C. Halfway up the stairs, the tall, dark-skinned lawyer glanced upward. He could see four familiar words carved across the front of the huge white building: Equal Justice Under Law. Marshall intended to make those words a reality.

Striding between the imposing columns, Marshall entered the vast sanctum of the United States Supreme Court. He laid his bulging briefcase on the table and drew a deep breath. Today, Marshall would offer his final arguments in the most important case of his distinguished career. If he won, the United States Supreme Court would rule that America's long-entrenched, segregated school systems were unconstitutional. If he lost, most of America's black children would continue to receive second-rate educations in substandard, ill-equipped schools.

Marshall's case, entitled *Brown v. Board of Education of Topeka*, was a consolidation of five separate lawsuits. Challenging the legality of their local school boards, black students and their parents had brought suits in Delaware, the District of Columbia, Kansas, South Carolina, and Virginia. The case of Virginia's 16-year-old Barbara Rose Johns was typical of the others. Dissatisfied with the only school open to her and other black students—a tar-paper shack lacking proper heat or other facilities—Johns had led 450 classmates in a strike that climaxed in legal action against the school board of Prince Edward County.

Marshall prepares to argue the most important case of his career: Brown v. Board of Education of Topeka. At stake in the 1952–54 U.S. Supreme Court case, which was a consolidation of five separate lawsuits challenging racial segregation in public schools, was the future of black education in the United States.

11

The South Carolina case involved gas station attendant Harry Briggs, a navy veteran from Clarendon County. Seeking improved school conditions for his 5 children, Briggs had joined 19 other black parents in a suit against the county's segregated school system. As a result, Briggs and his wife had lost their jobs and their credit at the local bank.

Defeated in each of the five locations, the black students and parents appealed to the Supreme Court. Because the Kansas case—in which Topeka parent Oliver Brown sued his city's school board—came first alphabetically, the five clustered cases came to be known as *Brown*. The case presented the court with a question of vital importance to millions of Americans: Is government-enforced school segregation unconstitutional?

When the segregation cases came before the Supreme Court, legal counsel, directed by attorney Thurgood Marshall, was supplied by the National Association for the Advancement of Colored People (NAACP). Founded in 1909, the NAACP—whose membership was biracial—had spent decades fighting racial discrimination and segregation. In its early years, the NAACP concentrated on obtaining black suffrage (the right to vote), eliminating lynching and other mob violence against blacks, and promoting integration in housing and public places.

By the early 1930s, NAACP officials realized that blacks could never achieve social and economic equality without educational equality, and the organization made improved schooling for blacks a top priority. Thurgood Marshall had joined the organization in 1934. Now, in 1953, the 45-year-old attorney hoped for a major victory in what had been a long, grueling struggle.

Marshall hoped to win the *Brown* case by demolishing the "separate but equal" doctrine established by *Plessy v. Ferguson*. A celebrated Supreme

Court case of 1896, *Plessy* began when a black man, Homer Adolph Plessy, refused to ride in the "Jim Crow" (segregated) car of a train passing through Louisiana. (The popular minstrel shows of the 19th century often featured white actors who wore black-face makeup and danced to the refrain, "Jump, Jim Crow!" The term Jim Crow, used as a patronizing name for black people, was also applied to post–Civil War segregation laws.)

Charged with violating a state law that required racial segregation in public facilities, Plessy was convicted by a Louisiana judge (Ferguson). When Plessy's lawyer appealed the conviction before the United States Supreme Court, he argued that enforced separation of the two races violated the Constitution's Fourteenth Amendment, which guarantees all citizens "the equal protection of the laws."

The Fourteenth Amendment was ratified in 1868, five years after President Abraham Lincoln's Emancipation Proclamation legally ended slavery in the South. The amendment was designed to guarantee newly freed blacks the same legal rights and privileges as whites. But the Supreme Court, in its 1896 *Plessy* decision, upheld the Louisiana segregation law, ruling that separate but "equal" facilities satisfied the amendment's "equal protection" guarantee.

Although the court's decision technically applied only to the Louisiana law, it established a *precedent* (a legal decision that serves as a rule or pattern for future, similar cases). When the Supreme Court establishes a precedent, the nation's lower courts are bound to follow it unless it is overturned by the Supreme Court itself. Because consistency is very important to a legal system, precedents are seldom overturned.

Plessy opened the gates for a flood of new Jim Crow laws—statutes that required racial separation in both private residential areas and public facilities.

Crowning the imposing Washington, D.C., building of the U.S. Supreme Court is the motto Equal Justice Under Law. But until the 1950s, when Marshall successfully argued that segregation was unconstitutional, many Americans acted as though the motto read Separate But Equal Justice Under Law.

Southern youngsters attend a one-room schoolhouse in the early 1950s. Until the U.S. Supreme Court outlawed segregation in 1954, most of the nation's black children had to enroll in racially separate, substandard schools.

By 1900, blacks in many states were restricted to Jim Crow drinking fountains, railroad cars, movie theater sections, hospitals, and schools. Despite the *Plessy* ruling, few state or local governments enforced the equality of the institutions and services available to blacks.

Guided by the separate-but-equal precedent, county and state courts routinely dismissed anti-segregation suits; black students could legally be compelled to attend segregated schools if these institutions were judged equal to the schools reserved for white students. The judgments, of course, were made by people committed to preserving the separation of the races. Segregation had become the law of the land.

To help him prepare his arguments in *Brown v. Board of Education of Topeka*, Marshall recruited dozens of experts: lawyers, constitutional scholars, sociologists, psychiatrists, anthropologists, and educators. Under Marshall's guidance, the team scrutinized all aspects of the Fourteenth Amendment, examined every available study of children's learning patterns, and pored over research on the history and psychological effects of segregation on youngsters of both races.

The Supreme Court agreed to hear the *Brown* case in its 1952 session. During the 1952 hearing, Marshall asserted that the whole weight of social science demonstrated that black and white children possessed equal learning potential. He pointed out that school segregation had no reasonable basis and that it had a devastating effect on black children, decreasing their motivation to learn, lowering their self-esteem, and blighting their futures.

The court's nine justices found Marshall's arguments impressive, but legal precedents were heavily stacked against the NAACP's position. Deciding that the issue bore further consideration, the justices scheduled a rehearing, which began on December 7, 1953. Now, on December 8, Thurgood Marshall would offer his final arguments in the case.

When Marshall entered the courtroom, spectators, both black and white, filled every seat. Eager to witness history, many had waited outside in the bitter cold since before daybreak. The crowd's excited murmurs ceased when the marshal of the court stepped forward and, in ringing tones, pronounced the ancient ritual words: "The honorable the Chief Justice, the Associate Justices of the Supreme Court of the United States. Oyez, oyez, oyez! All persons having business before the honorable the Supreme Court of the United States are advised to draw near and give their attention, for the Court is now sitting, and God save the United States and this honorable Court."

Everyone present stood and faced the long, highly polished bench at the front of the courtroom. Then the red velvet curtains behind the bench parted; nine black-robed men stepped forward and seated themselves in high-backed leather chairs.

Marshall eyed his opponent, John W. Davis. Tall, pale, and aristocratic in bearing, the 80-year-old Davis was known as the nation's leading constitutional lawyer. As a law student, Thurgood Marshall had sometimes skipped classes to hear Davis argue before the Supreme Court. By 1953, Davis had argued 140 cases before the high court. Marshall himself had participated in 15 Supreme Court cases, but *Brown* had brought him face-to-face with the formidable Davis for the first time.

Like Marshall, Davis argued *Brown* for moral rather than financial reasons. (His only payment for defending the South's segregated school systems, in fact, was a silver tea service, presented by the South Carolina legislature.) Davis believed segregation was not only fair but necessary. Marshall, of course, believed exactly the opposite, but he nevertheless respected the older attorney: John W. Davis was a force to be reckoned with, and Marshall knew it. Presenting his final points on the *Brown* case the day before, Davis had argued brilliantly. Although he referred to his notes more frequently than in the past, the elderly attorney had lost none of his eloquence. With his mane of snow-white hair and his formal, old-fashioned suit, he cut an impressive figure in the courtroom.

Davis regarded the separate-but-equal doctrine as a basic principle of American life. A time comes, he said, when such a principle "has been so often announced, so confidently relied upon, so long continued, that it passes the limits of judicial discretion and disturbance." Davis had no doubt that equality had been achieved in the segregated school system. "I am reminded," he said, "and I hope it won't be treated

as a reflection on anybody—of Aesop's fable of the dog and the meat: The dog, with a fine piece of meat in his mouth, crossed a bridge and saw [his] shadow in the stream and plunged in for it and lost both substance and shadow. Here is equal education, not promised, not prophesied, but present. Shall it be thrown away on some fancied question of racial prestige?"

Thurgood Marshall stepped up to the bar to make his final rebuttal. "I got the feeling on hearing the discussion yesterday that when you put a white child in a school with a whole lot of colored children, the child would fall apart or something," he said. "Everybody knows that is not true. These same kids in Virginia and South Carolina—and I have seen them

Marshall greets John W. Davis during the case of Brown v. Board of Education of Topeka. *America's foremost constitutional lawyer in the early 1950s, Davis argued 140 U.S. Supreme Court cases before Marshall defeated him in* Brown.

As the U.S. Supreme Court's pronouncement that "separate educational facilities are inherently unequal" makes headlines around the world, a mother and daughter celebrate the May 1954 overthrow of public-school segregation with a visit to the Supreme Court building.

do it—they play in the streets together, they play on their farms together, they go down the road together, they separate to go to school, they come out of school and play ball together. They have to be separated in school."

Marshall declared that school segregation laws were deliberately designed to oppress black people. The only way the Supreme Court could uphold them, he asserted, would be "to find that for some reason Negroes are inferior to all other human beings." Ending his argument, he said, "The only thing [segregation] can be is an inherent determination that the people who were formerly in slavery, regardless of anything else, shall be kept as near that stage as is possible. And now is the time, we submit, that this Court should make it clear that that is not what our Constitution stands for."

After the lawyers completed their arguments, the justices followed their standard procedure, conferring about the case in secret session. Five months later—on May 17, 1954—they reassembled at their great mahogany bench. As Chief Justice Earl Warren prepared to read the Court's opinion in *Brown v. Board of Education*, spectators leaned forward in silence. Wire-service reporters started filing their dispatches from the press table. At 12:57 P.M., the Associated Press wire carried a bulletin: "Chief Justice Warren today began reading the Supreme Court's decision in the public school desegregation cases. The court's ruling could not be determined immediately." The alarm went off in every newsroom in America. The nation waited.

But instead of delivering a crisp summary of the decision, Warren embarked on a long, discursive text. He referred to the evidence of psychologists, sociologists, and educators on the effects of segregation on black students. He discussed *Plessy v. Ferguson* and the Fourteenth Amendment's equal protection guarantee; thus far, he said, no precedent existed for the application of that guarantee to school segregation. After citing a number of earlier cases and outlining the history of black education in America, Warren called education "the most important function of state and local governments."

An hour after he started, the chief justice had yet to reveal the court's ruling. Warren, wired the AP correspondent at 1:12, "had not read far enough in the court's opinion for newsmen to say that segregation was being struck down as unconstitutional." Finally, at 1:20 P.M., Warren reached the crucial question: "Does segregation of children in public schools solely on the basis of race . . . deprive the children of the minority group of equal educational opportunities?"

Warren paused for a split second. Then he said, "We believe that it does." He continued: "To separate [black children] from others . . . solely because of their race generates a feeling of inferiority . . . that may affect their hearts and minds in a way unlikely ever to be undone."

Approaching the end of the decision, Warren read, "We conclude . . ." Then he paused, raised his eyes from the document, and added, "unanimously." A shock wave seemed to sweep the courtroom. The justice continued, ". . . that in the field of public education the doctrine of 'separate but equal' has no place. Separate educational facilities are inherently unequal."

Stop-press bulletins flashed across the land. Radio and TV stations interrupted their programming. The Voice of America network beamed the news across the world in 34 languages: The Supreme Court of the United States of America had declared school segregation unconstitutional. Word of the decision reached Thurgood Marshall and his colleague Roy Wilkins in the New York office of the NAACP. Decades of struggle had finally paid off in victory. Silently, the two campaign veterans embraced. ☙

Marshall with NAACP colleagues George E. C. Hayes (left) and James Nabrit (right), smiling victoriously outside the U.S. Supreme Court after educational segregation was declared unconstitutional. "I was so happy I was numb," Marshall said of the historic 1954 Supreme Court decision.

2

"A PRETTY TOUGH GUY"

❦

THURGOOD MARSHALL WAS born on July 2, 1908, in West Baltimore, Maryland. His combative nature seems to mirror that of his ancestors, especially his maternal great-grandfather, a slave brought to America in the mid-1800s. "His polite descendants like to think he came from the cultured tribes in Sierra Leone," Thurgood Marshall said, "but we all know that he really came from the toughest part of the Congo." (Until 1971, the Republic of Zaire was known as the Congo.)

According to Marshall, his great-grandfather "grew up into one mean man. One day his owner came up to him and said: 'Look, I brought you here so I guess I can't very well shoot you—as you deserve. On the other hand, I can't with a clear conscience sell anyone as vicious as you to another slaveholder. So, I'm going to set you free—on one condition. Get to hell out of this county and never come back.' " That, Marshall added, was "the only time Massuh didn't get an argument from the old boy." Marshall's great-grandfather raised no arguments, but he had no intention of complying with the slaveholder's wishes. He settled down and raised his family just a few miles from his former owner's plantation. "He lived there until the day he died," added Marshall, "and nobody ever laid a hand on him."

Marshall told this story to a *Time* magazine reporter in his characteristically easygoing, humorous style. But beneath the casual manner lay a familiarity

A snapshot from Marshall's family album shows the future civil rights activist as a toddler. Family members later described young Thurgood as a beautiful baby with silky hair and large, expressive eyes.

with the brutal facts of black bondage. Although African slavery had been practiced for centuries, the New World's demands for cheap labor vastly increased the traffic in human beings. Most slaves were captured from their villages by black tribal chiefs and brought to coastal markets. Sold to white ship captains, they were crammed aboard reeking ships and brought to America. Historians estimate that as many as half the slaves shipped from Africa died at sea, victims of malnutrition, disease, and outright murder. Some even took their own lives, preferring death to slavery.

Those slaves who survived the appalling voyage to the New World were sold at auction. Most of them became the property of southern plantation owners. Separated from their families, the enslaved Africans—men, women, and children—were put to work in the fields, laboring for 16 hours a day under constant vigilance and frequent abuse.

Beginning in the 18th century, southern states passed "black codes"—laws that forbade slaves to defend themselves against their masters' mistreatment, to own property, or to testify against whites in court. Under these codes, a white who taught a black to read or write was a criminal; a white who killed a black while punishing him, however, was acting legally. Marshall's Congolese great-grandfather, who refused to let these conditions defeat him, clearly filled his descendant with a powerful sense of family pride.

In the mid-19th century, many blacks in the United States used only one name, often that of their former owners. Another Thurgood Marshall ancestor—his paternal grandfather—was a freedman (former slave) known only as "Marshall." When Grandfather Marshall enlisted in the Union army during the Civil War, he learned that soldiers needed both first and last names. He chose to be called "Tho-

A group of USCTs—United States Colored Troops—line up at a Civil War military base. Marshall's grandfather Thoroughgood was one of the 186,000 former slaves who served in the Union armies.

roughgood" Marshall. "I was named after him," Thurgood Marshall told an interviewer, "but by the time I was in second grade, I got tired of spelling all that and shortened it."

After Union forces won the war, Thoroughgood Marshall spent several years in the United States merchant marine. Retiring from the sea, he married a woman named Annie and opened a grocery store in Baltimore. There, Annie Marshall fought and won her own small war. When Baltimore's electric company decided to install a light pole in front of the Marshalls' grocery store door, Annie Marshall objected. The sidewalk adjoining the store, she said, belonged to her and her husband, and they wanted no pole in the middle of it. After obtaining a court order, the company sent workmen to install the pole. When they got there, they found the site occupied by Annie Marshall, firmly seated in a kitchen chair. Day after day, the determined shopkeeper held her ground, finally forcing the company to find another site for its pole. Recounting the story with a smile, Thurgood Marshall said, "Grandma Annie emerged as the victor of what may have been the first successful sitdown strike in Maryland."

In a 1965 *Ebony* magazine interview, Marshall talked about his maternal grandfather, an opera-loving sailor named Isaiah Olive Branch Williams. As Thoroughgood Marshall had done, Williams served in the merchant marine, then married and settled down in Baltimore. But he never forgot a long-ago visit to Arica, a Chilean port where he had enjoyed a fine performance of Vincenzo Bellini's 1831 opera, *Norma*. When his wife gave birth to a daughter, Williams named the baby—Thurgood Marshall's mother—Norma Arica.

Now the head of a growing family, Williams bought a house in Baltimore. Unfortunately, his next-door neighbor turned out to be a bigoted white man who treated Williams with open contempt. When he needed Williams's help to mend the fence

Newly emancipated black families arrive in Baltimore in the 1860s. After the Civil War, both of Marshall's grandfathers opened grocery stores in the bustling Maryland city.

between the two properties, however, the neighbor changed his tune. "After all," he told Williams, "we belong to the same church and are going to the same heaven." Williams, the object of countless insults from his suddenly friendly neighbor, responded quickly. "I'd rather go to hell," he said.

Isaiah Williams also showed his assertiveness in the political sphere. In the 1870s, he organized a large public meeting to protest police brutality toward blacks. The rally produced no marked improvements, but it set a precedent, proving that Baltimore's usually passive black population could unite in a common cause. In the post–Civil War era, when white supremacist groups such as the Ku Klux Klan roamed the land, beating and sometimes murdering "uppity" blacks, any act of black defiance required extraordinary courage.

Isaiah Williams's daughter, Norma Arica, married William Canfield Marshall in 1904. The union produced two sons: William Aubrey, born in 1904, and Thurgood, who arrived four years later. The Marshalls lived on Druid Hill Avenue in West Baltimore, a middle-class neighborhood where black and white families coexisted in relative harmony. Druid Hill Avenue was a pleasant street lined with three-story brick row houses, each equipped with whitewashed front steps and an arched doorway.

When Thurgood was born, his father worked for the Baltimore & Ohio Railroad as a dining-car waiter. The job was a good one, especially for a black man at the turn of the century, but it kept Will Marshall away from his family for weeks at a time. Thus, when he got the chance to sign on as a waiter at the Gibson Island Club, he took it. Marshall eventually became chief steward at the club, a prestigious Chesapeake Bay sailing association whose members included powerful Washington politicians and social leaders.

Thurgood Marshall's mother, Norma Arica Marshall, taught in a segregated Baltimore elementary school. After graduating from an all-black Maryland college, she had earned graduate credits at Columbia University Teachers College in New York City. Like her father, Norma Marshall loved music. She was known as a talented pianist and singer and sometimes appeared in local opera and theater productions. Her sister-in-law, Elizabeth Marshall, recalled Norma as "a very strong person" and "a leader who went all out for her boys and had great influence on them."

According to his relatives, Thurgood was a beautiful baby with big, dark eyes. His aunt, Media Dodson, remembered him as a "timid" little boy. But, Dodson told a *Time* magazine reporter, "one day—he must have been around five—he stopped crying and became a pretty tough guy. Now, I don't know what caused the change. Maybe the boys slapped his head."

Whatever caused the change, Thurgood Marshall remained a "pretty tough guy." A *New York Times Magazine* story quotes him as saying, "We lived on a respectable street, but behind us there were back alleys where roughnecks and the tough kids hung out. When it was time for dinner, my mother used to go to the front door and call my older brother. Then she'd go to the *back* door and call me."

Reminiscing about young Thurgood, family friend Odell Payne told *Ebony* magazine that he "was a jolly boy who always had something to say." But, she added, Thurgood showed a serious side as well. "I can still see him coming down Division Street every Sunday afternoon about one o'clock," she said. "He'd be wearing knee pants with both hands dug way into his pockets and be kicking a stone in front of him as he crossed over to Dolphin Street to visit his grandparents at their big grocery store on the corner. He was in a deep study, that boy, and it was plain something was going on inside him."

But Thurgood's high-spirited side usually prevailed. His boisterous classroom behavior, in fact, often landed him in trouble. Thurgood's grade-school principal administered a standard punishment for rowdiness: banishment to the school basement with a copy of the United States Constitution. Not until he had memorized a passage from that document was the offender allowed to return to his class. "Before I left that school," Marshall later told a reporter, "I knew the whole thing by heart."

Parts of the Constitution, however, puzzled him. As an adult, Marshall remembered wondering about

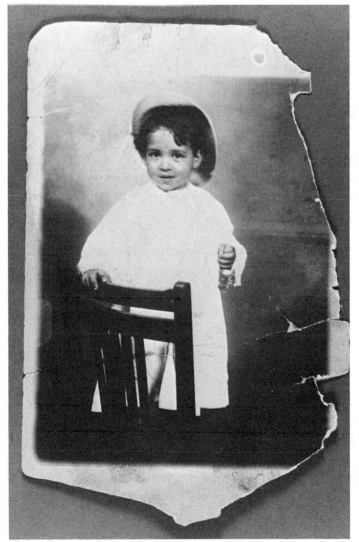

Two-year-old Thurgood's direct gaze gives a hint of the unflinching civil rights activist to come. One aunt, who described Marshall as a "timid" youngster, reported that by the age of five he had already become "a pretty tough guy."

Norma Arica Marshall, mother of Thurgood and William Aubrey Marshall, "went all out for her boys," according to one relative. A schoolteacher who demanded that her sons study hard, Norma Marshall lived to see the rewards of their labors: William became a prominent surgeon; Thurgood, a justice of the U.S. Supreme Court.

the Fourteenth Amendment's guarantee of "equal rights." Seeing inequality all around him, starting with his own segregated school, he asked his father what the guarantee meant. Will Marshall, recalled his son, simply said that the Constitution described things as they should be, not as they really were.

Thurgood Marshall's early acquaintance with the Constitution may have helped steer him toward the law, but his parents definitely influenced his future vocation. Will Marshall followed court cases as a hobby. He enjoyed reading newspaper accounts of impending trials, and he spent his occasional free afternoons in court, sometimes taking Thurgood with him.

In fact, William Marshall eventually became the first black to serve on a Baltimore grand jury. During his first two days on the jury, he observed that the jurors always asked whether the person under investigation was white or black. Blacks, he noted, were far more likely to be indicted (charged with a crime) than whites. On his third day as a juror, Marshall suggested that the jury drop the question of race when it was considering potential guilt or innocence. His words produced a tense silence in the jury room. Then, to Marshall's surprise, the white foreman agreed with him. That particular grand jury never again raised the question of race.

Although Will Marshall had received little formal education, he had an analytical mind and loved to debate. Thurgood Marshall later told a writer from U.S. News & World Report that it was his father who steered him toward a legal career. "He never told me to become a lawyer, but he turned me into one," said Marshall. "He did it by teaching me to argue, by challenging my logic on every point, by making me prove every statement I made."

Norma Marshall wanted her son to be a dentist, not a lawyer. Nevertheless, she helped him develop attitudes and skills that would prove useful in the career he chose. A bright student, Thurgood could have coasted through school, getting good grades with very little effort. But Norma Marshall put a high priority on education. She insisted that her son work hard and use his mind to its full capacity. According to Aubrey Marshall, Thurgood—like the boys' father—tended to be "very argumentive and aggressive." Norma Marshall's personality formed a sharp contrast. Conciliatory and diplomatic, she helped counteract Thurgood's sometimes tactless and impatient manner.

Norma and Will Marshall could provide their son with a secure and affectionate home, but they could not shelter him from prejudice against blacks. Marshall never forgot the day he discovered racism. Years later, he told a *Time* magazine reporter about the experience:

> I heard a kid call a Jewish boy I knew a "kike" to his face. I was about seven. I asked him why he didn't fight the kid. He asked me what would I do if somebody called me "nigger"—would I fight? That was a new one on me. I knew kike was a dirty word, but I hadn't known about nigger. I went home and wanted to know right that minute what all this meant. That's not easy for a parent to explain so it makes any sense to a kid, you know.

Although Will Marshall found it hard to define the word, he had no difficulty in telling his son how to react to it. "Anyone calls you nigger," he told Thurgood, "you not only got my permission to fight him—you got my orders to fight him."

A few years later, Thurgood Marshall followed those orders. By then a high school student, he led a busy life, managing to get excellent grades while participating in school clubs, going out for several sports, attending frequent dances, and, after school, delivering supplies for a hat company. One afternoon, he recalled later, he was carrying a stack of hatboxes

Thurgood Marshall's father, William, made his position on racism clear to his son. "Anyone calls you nigger," he told young Thurgood, "you not only got my permission to fight him—you got my orders to fight him."

so high he "couldn't see over them." Waiting for a trolley, he met and chatted with one of his father's friends, a man named Truesdale.

When the trolley arrived, Marshall arranged the bulky hatboxes as best he could and carefully stepped up to the platform. Suddenly, he felt himself seized by the arm and yanked backwards. "Nigguh, don't you push in front of no white lady again," snarled a male voice. "I hadn't seen any white lady," recalled Marshall, "so I tore into him. The hats scattered all over the street." The white man lunged back at Marshall, and the two were soon engaged in noisy battle.

Truesdale tried without success to break up the fight. At last, a policeman arrived and separated the combatants. The peacemaker turned out to be Army Matthews, a white neighborhood police officer known to be racially tolerant. Instead of automatically assuming that Marshall, because he was black, was at fault in the dispute, Matthews asked Truesdale for an eyewitness account. A deferential black man who preferred to avoid racial confrontations, Truesdale first apologized for Marshall's actions, then explained how the fight had started. After listening carefully, Matthews escorted both contestants to the police station. Charging neither with an offense, he dismissed them shortly afterward.

For a black man, striking—or even talking back to—a white man was dangerous business in the early 20th century, especially in a southern state. Truesdale's humble, apologetic manner exemplified what most whites expected—and got—from most blacks. Marshall's furious response to his white challenger might have earned him a savage beating, a jail sentence, or worse. Thanks to Army Matthews, the incident ended peacefully, but white policemen willing to listen to a black's version of an interracial squabble were rare. Marshall had been courageous. He had also been very lucky.

Despite Marshall's readiness to stand up for his rights, he sometimes had to compromise. Soon after his run-in at the trolley stop, he faced another challenge, this one less threatening but still uncomfortable. It started when his father helped him get a high school vacation job as a waiter on the Baltimore & Ohio Railroad. On the teenager's first day at work, the chief dining-car steward gave him a pair of waiter's pants. Finding them too short, the tall, lanky Marshall asked for another pair. "Boy," said the steward, "we can get a man to fit the pants a lot easier than we can get pants to fit the man. Why don't you scroonch down a little more?"

Marshall assessed the situation. Most work open to blacks, especially to male black teenagers, involved straight menial labor; a job on the B & O was a bonanza, not to be taken lightly, especially because he needed money for his education. Recalling the incident with a chuckle, he reported his next move: "I scroonched."

Although the adult Thurgood Marshall was able to joke about such incidents, growing up black—and ambitious—in early 20th-century America was no laughing matter. But even in that era of overt racism, Marshall grew up with a strong sense of dignity and self-respect. From his early years, he took pride in his family, starting with the tough-minded great-grandfather who fought his way out of slavery. Like his ancestors, Thurgood Marshall intended to claim his own position in American society.

3

THE EXTRA STEP

THURGOOD MARSHALL GRADUATED from high school in 1925, determined to continue his education. His parents, who had already managed to send their firstborn son to college, backed Thurgood's ambition enthusiastically. Aubrey Marshall, by this point a medical student, would become an eminent chest surgeon. Norma Marshall still hoped to make a dentist of her younger son.

In the 1920s, the United States offered its college-bound black students few choices. White colleges in the South were forbidden by law to accept blacks; white colleges in other parts of the country accepted very few. Thurgood Marshall decided to apply to one of the nation's all-black institutions. He chose Lincoln University, the nation's oldest black college.

Founded by a Presbyterian clergyman and his wife in 1854, Lincoln was chartered to provide "for the scientific, classical, and theological education of colored youth of the male sex." Although the distinguished Pennsylvania college is now open to students of all races and both sexes, its enrollment was all male and all black when Marshall entered. Specializing in liberal arts and teacher education, Lincoln sent about half of its alumni to graduate schools where they studied medicine, dentistry, education, and the law.

The college attracted a highly cosmopolitan group of young men, drawing its students from all sections of the United States and from such distant points as Africa and Asia. Among Thurgood Marshall's classmates were two future presidents of African nations:

Like other black high school graduates in the 1920s, 17-year-old Marshall faced limited educational options. Barred from the nation's exclusively white institutions, he selected Pennsylvania's distinguished Lincoln University, America's oldest black college.

Kwame Nkrumah of Ghana and Nnamdi Azikiwe of Nigeria. Another fellow student was Cabell Calloway, a young singer from Rochester, New York, who would later earn international fame as bandleader Cab Calloway.

Like countless college freshmen before him, Marshall played harder than he worked during his first semesters. The future lawyer became a charter member of the Weekend Club, a group of fun-loving students who swore they would never be found on campus over a weekend. True to his promise, Marshall used up his whole year's allowance of excused absences during his first semester. And when he was on campus, he later confessed, he spent most of his spare time playing cards. In his sophomore year, he and a group of friends were suspended for hazing new students, although they managed to shave several freshman heads before college officals caught them. "I got the horsin' around out of my system," Marshall said later.

Despite his antics, Marshall managed to maintain a B average and to read an impressive number of books. He was especially intrigued by the writings of W. E. B. Du Bois, the celebrated black scholar and activist who wrote *The Souls of Black Folk*, a searing collection of essays on black life, and edited the *Crisis*, the nation's largest black periodical. Published by the NAACP, the *Crisis* was renowned for Du Bois's powerful editorials.

Marshall was also exposed to the outpouring of black literature during the Harlem Renaissance. The 1920s, a time of general prosperity in America, produced a dazzling array of art from the New York City district of Harlem, the nation's unofficial black capital. Among the authors whose works appeared during Marshall's college years were poets Claude McKay, Countee Cullen, Jean Toomer, and Langston Hughes, perhaps the first major black poet whose writing specifically addressed members of his own

A founding member of the NAACP, William Edward Burghardt Du Bois spearheaded the fight for black equality in the first half of the 20th century. His long tenure at the NAACP's New York office briefly overlapped that of Marshall, who as a college student had been deeply impressed by The Souls of Black Folk *and other Du Bois works.*

race. Absorbed by the literature and social commentaries published by contemporary black authors, Marshall began to contemplate the role of the black individual in American society. It was a subject he would study for the rest of his life.

Marshall's college activities also included politics and protest. One evening, he and a group of friends decided to integrate the movie theater in nearby Oxford, Pennsylvania. When they bought their tickets, the seller sternly reminded them of the theater's rules: Black patrons were restricted to the balcony. Ignoring the reminder, the students marched into the theater and took seats in the "whites only" orchestra section.

An usher immediately ordered them to move to the balcony. When they stayed put, the usher loudly repeated his command, but the black students just gazed intently at the western on the screen. Then Marshall felt someone breathing on the back of his neck. "Nigger," said a harsh male voice, "why don't you just get out of here and sit where you belong?" Marshall quietly told the man that he had paid for his ticket and intended to stay where he was. Describing the episode in a letter to his family, he said, "You can't really tell what a person like that looks like because it's just an ugly feeling that's looking at you, not a real face."

Marshall's letter went on to report the incident's conclusion: "We found out that they only had one fat cop in the whole town and they wouldn't have the nerve or the room in the jail to arrest all of us. But the amazing thing was, when we were leaving, we just walked out with all those other people and they didn't do anything, didn't say anything, didn't even look at us—at least, not as far as I know. I'm not sure I like being invisible, but maybe it's better than being put to shame and not able to respect yourself."

During his college years, Marshall sometimes attended Philadelphia's Cherry Street Memorial

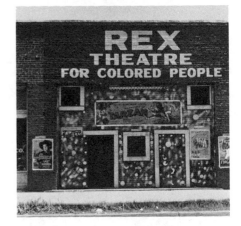

Until the 1950s, the South restricted its black residents to such separate facilities as this segregated movie theater in Leland, Mississippi. In the North, black moviegoers were usually obliged to sit in the balcony, called "nigger heaven" by patronizing whites.

Church with his friends. "We went in there because we learned that's where all the cute chicks went," he joked later. The "cute chick" he met was Vivian Burey, a University of Pennsylvania undergraduate. The two students fell in love almost immediately. "First we decided to get married five years after I graduated, then three, then one, and we finally did just before I started my last semester," Marshall recalled later.

Marshall and Burey, both 21 years old, were married on September 4, 1929. The Lincoln senior and his bride, who had already received her college degree, moved into a small apartment in Oxford. To help finance his education, both husband and wife worked: Thurgood Marshall as a bellhop and waiter and Vivian Marshall—whom everyone called "Buster"—as a secretary. According to friends, Buster Marshall exerted a stabilizing influence on her high-spirited young husband. "She helped 'turn him around' and inspired in him an academic zeal," said one observer.

Thurgood Marshall had enjoyed debates ever since his early discussions with his father. Known as "the Wrathful Marshall," he became the star of Lincoln's Forensic Society, leading the debating team to a string of impressive victories. In his senior year, dismayed by Lincoln's calamitous 1929 football season, Marshall reportedly jumped onto the stage during a pregame rally and delivered a fiery 20-minute pep talk. Ignited by his blazing rhetoric, the Lincoln football squad rushed onto the field and played its finest game of the year. The inspired performance produced only a scoreless tie, but Marshall cheerfully took credit for it. In any case, he had demonstrated the oratorical skill that would one day distinguish him in the courts.

In June 1930, Marshall received his A.B. degree, with honors in the humanities (literature, philosophy, and the arts). His interest in becoming a dentist,

Marshall (middle row, second from right) and his fellow Lincoln University freshmen sit for a class portrait in 1925. In spite of his mother's early guidance, Marshall earned a college reputation for being, as one friend later put it, "something of a playboy."

never strong, had steadily diminished during his college years. He was a gifted, persuasive speaker, and he enjoyed facing an audience. By the time he graduated, he had decided to enter the law. It was a decision he never regretted.

When Norma and Will Marshall invited their son and his wife to share their home in Baltimore, the young couple accepted quickly. They knew they needed to save every penny for law school. Norma Marshall, at last persuaded that law was a better choice for her son than dentistry, even sold her engagement ring to help pay his tuition expenses. Marshall applied to the University of Maryland's law school, a highly regarded Baltimore institution. The all-white university had never accepted a black student, and its administrators had no intention of changing its policy for Thurgood Marshall. They turned him down immediately.

Marshall next turned to Howard University's law school, which accepted his application. Founded in 1867 as a school for newly freed slaves, the Washington, D.C., institution had grown steadily in size and prestige. When Marshall entered law school in 1930, most of Howard's student body was black, although the college accepted students of all races and both sexes. Then as now, a large proportion of the nation's black doctors, dentists, engineers, architects, and lawyers held degrees from Howard.

Students stroll across the Washington, D.C., campus of Howard University, where Marshall attended the law school. Established in 1867 for young black males, Howard later opened its doors to men and women of all races.

Remembering his first week at law school, Marshall said he knew that "this was it. This was what I wanted to do for as long as I lived." Although he had been known, according to one old friend, as "something of a playboy" at Lincoln, Marshall changed his ways at Howard. He sped through his first year at a frantic pace. Up every day at 5:30 A.M., he caught a train to Washington, attended classes until 3 o'clock in the afternoon, boarded the return train to Baltimore, and then reported for his part-time job. After dinner with his wife and parents, he studied until midnight. "I heard law books were to dig in," he once recalled, "so I dug, way deep."

The long days took their toll on the young law student, whose weight fell from 170 to 130 pounds. But his hard work paid off. At the end of his first year, he was named top student in his class, an achievement that brought him the coveted job of assistant in Howard's law library. The position paid enough to keep him in law school, but it also kept him in Washington until 10 o'clock every night. In spite of his backbreaking schedule, however, Marshall acquired a large circle of friends and kept up an active social life. One law school classmate remembered him as "a dual personality. On the one hand, serious, and on the other hand, crazy." Marshall "was happy-go-lucky on the face of it," recalled another law school friend, "but he managed to get a lot of work done when nobody was looking."

When Marshall entered Howard, Mordecai Johnson, its first black president, was in the process of revolutionizing the school. Eager to promote what he called "higher individualism," Johnson rebuilt the college campus, expanded its curriculum, hired an impressive array of new instructors, and raised the university's academic standing to new heights. Johnson later credited a white friend, Supreme Court justice Louis Brandeis, with helping to inspire the transformation. "[Brandeis] told me that the one thing I should do was to build a law school and train men to get the constitutional rights of our people," Johnson recalled. "He said, 'Once you train lawyers to do this, the Supreme Court will have to hand your people their civil and constitutional rights.' "

Among the outstanding staff members recruited by Johnson was law professor William Henry Hastie, a Harvard graduate who later became the first black federal judge as well as a close friend and NAACP associate of Thurgood Marshall's. Another leading Howard figure was Charles Hamilton Houston, a brilliant attorney and pioneering civil rights activist. Appointed vice-dean of Howard's law school in 1929, Houston had remained active in the NAACP. He taught his students how to research and structure their cases, how to use existing laws to fight racial injustice, and how to act as "social engineers" as well as lawyers. Houston, who quickly spotted Marshall as a superior candidate for the law, paid special attention to the young student from Baltimore. And Marshall, recalled a law school contemporary, "idolized Charlie."

"Harvard was training people to join big law firms; Howard was teaching lawyers to go to court," Marshall told an interviewer years afterward. "Charlie's phrase was Social Engineer. He wanted us to be a part of the community. He wanted the lawyer to take over the leadership in the community." Part of Marshall's training under Houston and Hastie consisted of late-night sessions at which the lawyers plotted strategies for their current NAACP cases. Walter White, then chief executive of the NAACP, attended one such session. White was impressed by Marshall, whom he described as "a lanky, brash young senior law student who was always present," but he was also "amazed at [Marshall's] assertiveness in challenging positions [taken] by Charlie [Houston] and the other lawyers." However, added White, "I soon learned of his great value to the case in doing everything he was asked."

Charles Hamilton Houston taught Marshall in law school, worked with him on his first cases, and later hired him as NAACP counsel. "What Charlie beat into our heads," said Marshall later, "was excellence."

During their night sessions in the library, Marshall and his colleagues worked out legal research problems, some of them proposed by Houston, others by the students themselves. One evening, Marshall recalled later, "one guy started to work on something and we all joined in. And we found out that in codifying the Code of the District of Columbia, they had just left out the Civil Rights statute. Since it didn't apply to anyone but us, they left it out. We eventually got through the court and got that straightened out."

In 1932, Professor Hastie asked Marshall, then a second-year law student, to help prepare a *brief* (a written argument presented to a court by a lawyer) in a North Carolina desegregation case. The action involved a black college graduate who had been refused admission to the University of North Carolina law school because of his color. Claiming that his rejection violated the Constitution's equal protection guarantee, the applicant sued the university. He lost the case, then asked Hastie to handle an *appeal*: When a *litigant* (a person engaged in a lawsuit) loses in court, he or she may request the next higher court—the court of appeals—to review the case. The appeals court judge reads briefs from both sides before hearing the lawyers' oral arguments.

Despite Hastie and Marshall's carefully constructed brief, they lost their case in the North Carolina appeals court. The University of North Carolina was state supported, but its students paid tuition. Therefore, the court ruled, the university could be considered a private institution, under no obligation to extend equal rights to its applicants. This precedent has since been overturned.

Although Marshall met defeat in the North Carolina case, Howard and its professors taught him a great deal about the actual practice of law. Many law schools, even today, emphasize legal philosophy and history rather than hands-on experience. But at Howard, as Marshall later put it, "The emphasis was not on theory; the emphasis in this school was on practice, on how to get it done." Addressing Howard students many years after his own graduation, Marshall praised both the college and his mentor, Charles Houston. "[What] Charlie beat into our heads," said Marshall, "was excellence. He said, 'When a doctor makes a mistake, he buries his mistake. When a lawyer makes a mistake, he makes it in front of God and everybody else.' "

Thurgood Marshall had taken his training at Howard Law School to heart. In the same address, he endorsed the school's demand for hard work: "When you get in a courtroom, you can't just say, 'Please, Mr. Court, have mercy on me because I'm a Negro.' You are in competition with a well-trained white lawyer and you better be at least as good as he is; and if you expect to win, you better be better. If I give you five cases to read overnight, you better read eight. And when I say eight, you read ten. You go that step further; and you might make it."

As a law student, Marshall took that "step further": In 1933, he graduated first in his class. Harvard University immediately offered him a postgraduate scholarship, but he declined. It was a handsome tribute to his abilities, but Marshall had worked long and hard for the right to practice law. Now that he had his degree, that was exactly what he intended to do. He took the bar examination (a test required by each state before it allows a lawyer to practice) in Maryland, passed it with flying colors, and opened an office in Baltimore. Thurgood Marshall was on his way. ✿

Judge William Henry Hastie (right) chats with members of a youth group in Louisville, Kentucky, in the 1940s. One of Marshall's professors and friends at Howard University, Hastie became the nation's first black federal judge in 1949.

4

FIGHTING
THE ODDS

THURGOOD MARSHALL MOVED into a small office in east Baltimore, hung out a sign, hired a secretary, and waited for business. In 1933, when Marshall began his practice, black lawyers were scarce; the ratio of black citizens to black attorneys in the United States stood at 200,000 to 1. Fewer than a dozen black lawyers practiced in Baltimore, a city with thousands of black residents. Despite their rarity, however, these lawyers faced formidable odds against success.

In the first decades of the 20th century, a black citizen who hoped to win a lawsuit, especially a suit against a white defendant, generally hired a white attorney. At a time when almost all judges and juries were white, and when many of those white people harbored racial prejudices, a white attorney clearly had a better chance of success than a black attorney. "Negroes weren't anxious to have Negro lawyers," recalled a colleague of Marshall's. "The feeling was that whites could get more for them . . . and the white lawyers, frankly, fed the feeling." Virtually the only black Americans who sought out attorneys of their own race were those without the funds to pay for legal services.

The state of America's economy added to the obstacles confronting Marshall and other black attorneys of the time. The Great Depression, triggered by the stock market crash of 1929, had reached its peak by the mid-1930s. Because few individuals of any race could afford to go to court, the entire legal

When Marshall opened his own law office in 1933, he got off to a slow start. In those days, recalled a black associate, "Negroes weren't anxious to have Negro lawyers. The feeling was that whites could get more for them."

43

profession suffered. Hardest hit, of course, were the already struggling black lawyers.

Marshall had not expected to become rich when he opened his office, but he had hoped for a few paying clients. During his first year as a lawyer, he had none. Rather than making money, in fact, he lost it: His books for his first 12 months of practice showed a net loss of $1,000, a sizable sum in 1933. Years later, Marshall told a reporter about his early days as a lawyer: "One day I'd bring two lunches and the next day, my secretary would bring two lunches and sometimes we'd be the only two people in that office for weeks at a time."

Clients finally began to appear: tenants evicted for nonpayment of rent, people who had received large penalties for small infractions of the law, or victims of police brutality. Very few could afford even modest legal fees, but Marshall turned no one away. He soon earned a reputation as "the little man's lawyer."

Years later, Marshall smiled as he told the story of an elderly black farm woman who had moved from South Carolina to Baltimore. Back home, the woman had received free legal advice from the county judge, but when she sought counsel from a Baltimore judge, he told her to get in touch with Thurgood Marshall. As she later confessed to Marshall, "He said you was a freebie lawyer."

Marshall, who prepared for each trial with painstaking care, won many of his early cases. The parade of needy clients passing through his door brought him no money, but it did help him polish his courtroom style. Poet Langston Hughes later described Marshall as a persuasive man who "has moved many a judge to search his conscience and come up with decisions he probably did not know he had in him." Another Marshall observer commented, "He is an effective lawyer because he has common sense and a good instinct for facts."

Marshall's *pro bono* (public service) work provided more than hands-on experience. As author Richard Kluger noted in his 1976 book, *Simple Justice*, "It was only a matter of time before word spread about [Marshall's] competence as well as his generosity of spirit. In effect, provision of his services *gratis* [free] or close to it was the best (and only) advertisement a struggling black attorney could have. . . . He began to pick up some solid clients."

Among Marshall's new, paying accounts were a large Baltimore laundry, several labor associations, and Carl Murphy, head of Baltimore's wealthiest and most influential black family. As publisher of a popular weekly newspaper, the *Afro-American*, Murphy had long backed the slowly expanding civil rights movement. Thus, when Lillie Jackson, a middle-aged Baltimore housewife, decided to reactivate the local chapter of the NAACP in 1934, she asked Murphy to bankroll the membership drive. Murphy promised his support, then chose Marshall to act as the chapter's lawyer. Like most of Marshall's jobs, the position of NAACP counsel paid nothing. For the young lawyer, however, the honor of working for the city's leading black-rights group was compensation enough.

Because the NAACP's Baltimore branch had dwindled to a mere handful of members, Marshall, Jackson, and Murphy began a vigorous campaign to revive local interest. Some potential recruits had been skeptical of the organization because of its reputation for admitting only the black elite. As Marshall put it, "When I was a kid, we used to say that NAACP stood for the National Association for the Advancement of *Certain* People." But now things would be different. Marshall visited every black neighborhood in town, talking to individuals, making speeches to crowds, and explaining how much a unified community could accomplish.

Richard Kluger discussed Marshall's early NAACP activities with the Reverend A. J. Payne,

Displaying a photograph of a lynching, an NAACP poster asks: "Can you look at this picture and refuse to help?" Marshall, who began working for the NAACP in 1934, devoted almost three decades to the black-rights organization.

then pastor of a large Baptist church in Baltimore. "The prevailing feeling here then among too many was that segregation was segregation, and it was going to be that way till kingdom come," Payne said. "Some very fine men in the community were just plain afraid. Young Marshall, though, was different. He showed his courage and his tenacity, and the people liked him, the common people and the professional people both. . . . He'd say that, Jim Crow or no Jim Crow, we were free citizens and as such we had rights but we were going to have to fight to get them. People in the community looked up to him. He was never arrogant and always accessible."

Briscoe Koger, a black Baltimore attorney, shared Payne's sentiments about Marshall: "Old-timers had

Following southern custom, North Carolinians quench their thirst at separate drinking fountains in 1945. Not until 1961 would Americans be able to travel without seeing "white" and "colored" signs in railroad stations and bus depots.

the feeling that here finally was a leader. Everybody was in his corner. Others had none of the assurance and power that whites were accustomed to, but Thurgood Marshall had that."

Marshall kicked off his NAACP career by leading a boycott of stores on Baltimore's Pennsylvania Avenue. Although they depended on black customers, the white owners of these shops flatly refused to hire any black workers. Marshall and his colleagues persuaded a group of unemployed black high-school graduates to form picket lines outside the stores, urging shoppers to stay away until the merchants changed their hiring policies. Sales plummeted, but instead of compromising, the shopkeepers sued the NAACP.

Marshall's Howard University mentor, Charles Houston, joined his protégé in defending the suit. The two lawyers worked as a team, Marshall researching the case and Houston presenting it in court. The spectators who packed Baltimore's federal courthouse during the trial gasped when the white judge announced his verdict: He not only ruled in favor of the NAACP but congratulated Marshall and Houston on their effective presentation.

Working with Lillie Jackson, Marshall next embarked on an NAACP campaign to organize Maryland's black schoolteachers. Like their counterparts throughout the South, the black teachers received much lower salaries than white teachers. The only way to correct the problem, asserted Marshall and Jackson, was through legal action. But most of the black teachers, afraid of being laid off, hesitated to sue their school boards. The NAACP team finally overcame the teachers' reluctance by raising money for an emergency fund to pay any teachers who lost their jobs. Although it took several years, the drive eventually succeeded. Its first beneficiary was a Maryland county school principal whose annual salary rose from $612 to $1,475 as the result of an NAACP-backed lawsuit.

In the 1930s, black Americans faced social injustice, segregation, and discrimination on numerous fronts, including education, criminal justice, voting, housing, recreational facilities, and public accommodations. With limited funds and personnel, the NAACP had to hit the most vulnerable targets first. Its executives, who regarded higher education as the "soft underbelly" of southern segregation, decided to concentrate their forces on graduate schools.

White resistance to integrated public schools formed a virtually unbreakable wall. Resistance to integration on the graduate and professional level, the NAACP believed, might be easier to overcome. Graduate students were far fewer in number than public school students, and systematic segregation at the graduate school level would be relatively simple to demonstrate. And Marshall and his colleagues believed that judges, who were lawyers themselves, might quickly grasp the argument that "separate" law schools could never be "equal." NAACP officials also believed that victory in a small number of cases would establish legal precedents that could eventually be applied to all black educational opportunities. By the mid-1930s, the NAACP had committed itself to an all-out attack on discrimination in law schools.

Joining Charles Houston in the first battle, Marshall scored his first major court victory in 1935. The case, *Murray v. Pearson*, pitted a 20-year-old black college graduate, Donald Gaines Murray, against the University of Maryland and its president, Raymond A. Pearson. When Murray applied to the university's law school, Pearson rejected him. Murray, he asserted, could obtain "separate but equal" training at the Princess Anne Academy, a segregated institution on Maryland's Eastern Shore.

Pointing out that the academy offered no legal degree, Murray renewed his application to the Maryland law school. "The university," responded Pearson, "does not accept Negro students." Murray then

Marshall (left) and Charles Houston (right) work with Donald Gaines Murray on their 1935 suit against the University of Maryland. Thanks to Marshall and Houston, Murray became the first black admitted to the law school at the previously all-white university.

took the university to court. Arguing his case, Marshall and Houston once again worked as a team, dividing up the research and the court presentation.

Murray came to trial in June 1935. Armed with Marshall's meticulously assembled precedents and arguments, Houston demolished the opposition. He forced Pearson to admit that Princess Anne Academy lacked the facilities, the faculty, and the educational resources of the University of Maryland; that Murray was fully qualified for admission to the university; and that the University of Maryland law school was the only institution at which Murray could receive training in Maryland law.

Presenting the final arguments of the case, Marshall demonstrated his mastery of constitutional law. The "separate" part of the separate-but-equal doctrine, he noted, had been upheld by the Supreme Court, but the "equal" part had never been tested. Now that the defendants had conceded that the separate facilities offered Murray were unequal, argued Marshall, the court had no choice but to order the university to admit him. "What's at stake here is more than the rights of my client," he said. "It's the moral commitment stated in our country's creed." Listening

An official at the NAACP's Manhattan headquarters points to the group's latest recruitment poster. When NAACP special counsel Charles Houston recruited Marshall as his assistant and told him that the job involved frustration and danger, Marshall took it without hesitation.

to his impassioned words were three especially attentive courtroom spectators: Norma, Will, and Buster Marshall.

Marshall and Houston's combined eloquence won the day. On June 25, the Baltimore City Court ordered Pearson to admit Donald Murray to the university law school at once. Marshall appeared calm and somber as he heard the verdict, but when he left the courtroom with his wife and parents, he expressed his real feelings: Seizing Buster Marshall in his arms, he swept her off her feet in a jubilant tango.

The university appealed the decision, but without success. "Whatever system is adopted for legal education now," ruled the Maryland Court of Appeals, "must furnish equality of treatment now." Donald Murray entered the University of Maryland law school without incident, earned his degree, and opened a practice in Baltimore. Throughout his career, he made his legal services available to the NAACP without charge.

Marshall continued to rally Maryland's teachers and to work toward improved public schools for black children. His personal financial picture, however, failed to improve. In a better economic climate, his nonpaying NAACP work might have been balanced by profitable private practice, but the depression still gripped the land, and Marshall still represented people who could not afford to pay him. Then, in 1936, he got a call from Charles Houston. The former Howard University dean, now first special counsel to the NAACP, invited Marshall to become his assistant at a salary of $2,400 per year. Houston told Marshall that the job would be sometimes discouraging, often frustrating, and usually dangerous. Marshall accepted immediately.

For the next two years, Marshall and Houston worked together closely, spending much of their time traveling from one southern courthouse to another as they filed lawsuits for black students and teachers. Talking to Richard Kluger about those days, Marshall recalled that "Charlie would sit in my car—I had a little old beat-up '29 Ford—and type out the briefs. And he could type up a storm—faster than any secretary—and not just with two fingers going. I mean he used 'em all." Because accommodations for black travelers in the South of the 1930s were either dismal or nonexistent, the two attorneys spent most of their nights with friends. Assisting Houston meant long days of nonstop labor for Marshall. "He used to work like hell and way into the night," recalled a former aide.

When he was not on the road with Houston, Marshall divided his time between New York City—headquarters of the NAACP—and Baltimore. Unwilling to abandon his many poor clients, he kept a small office in his family's home, attending to his townspeople's needs until, as he later put it, "they adjusted over to new lawyers." In 1936, he handled his first case as NAACP assistant special counsel. Another law school suit, this one involved black college graduate Lloyd Gaines, who had applied to the law school at the University of Missouri. Rejecting him on the basis of his race, the university offered to pay his tuition at an out-of-state law school. This policy, asserted the state of Missouri, complied with the separate-but-equal doctrine. Not so, said the NAACP, which called the policy unconstitutional, a violation of the Fourteenth Amendment.

Represented by Houston, who argued the case, and Marshall, who wrote the all-important brief, Gaines sued the state of Missouri. In November 1938, after a series of Missouri courts had ruled against Gaines, the Supreme Court agreed to hear the case. Marshall based his brief on the Fourteenth Amendment's "equal protection of the laws" section. Rather than challenging the separate-but-equal doctrine, the brief demanded equality: If Missouri refused to admit Gaines to its all-white law school, it must offer him— and other qualified black applicants—equal facilities within the state. By a vote of six to two, the Supreme Court agreed with the Marshall-Houston argument. State laws that called for segregation, ruled the court, were permissible only when they provided the separated races with equal privileges within the state. Because Missouri had failed to supply a separate-but-equal law school for blacks, the state was obliged to let Gaines enter the only law school available, the hitherto all-white University of Missouri.

The Gaines case had far-reaching implications. In effect, the Court said Missouri could maintain separate law schools for both races, but only if those schools were truly equal. Missouri—and other states—now faced two alternatives: integrating their law schools or building and staffing brand-new law schools for blacks, a crushingly expensive proposition. Elated NAACP officials realized that one day the Supreme Court's reinforcement of the separate-but-equal doctrine might extend to public schools at all levels, as well as to teachers' salaries and student facilities across the nation. Thurgood Marshall had helped breach a mighty wall.

In late 1938, Charles Houston resigned as NAACP special counsel because of ill health. Marshall, 30 years old, replaced him. With his wife, he moved into a walk-up apartment in Harlem and took over Houston's desk at the NAACP's lower Fifth Avenue headquarters. As chief counsel to the important civil rights organization, Marshall had become black America's most prominent attorney. But his personal style— relaxed, informal, and down-to-earth—remained unchanged.

Taking stock of the New York office, Marshall found it far too "tush-tush," as he put it, for his tastes. "It was Dr. Whoosis and Mr. Whatsis and all kind of nonsense like that, bowing and scraping like an embassy scene," he later told a *New York Times* reporter. "Well, I took a long look," he continued, "and I figured I'd have to bust that stuff up pretty quick. Believe me, I had them talking first names in nothing time and no more of that formality business." Describing his boss, an NAACP aide later said, "Thurgood was always one of the gang. He never put barriers between himself and the less exalted."

Soon after he took over as NAACP special counsel, Marshall traveled to Dallas, Texas, to investigate a recent incident of racial violence. It centered on a 65-year-old black man, the president of a local junior college, who had received a notice to report for jury duty. When he appeared at the Dallas courthouse, appalled officials discovered they had summoned a black man and told him to go home. The educator, however, insisted on exercising his rights as a citizen. Enraged, two white court workers grabbed the frail, elderly man, dragged him out of the jury room, and threw him down the courthouse steps.

The college president survived, but the episode sparked flames of hostility among both blacks and whites. By the time Marshall arrived in town, Dallas seethed with rage. Marshall appraised the situation, then called on Texas governor James Allred. Amazed that a black attorney from New York dared to come to Texas and explain the law to him, the governor gave Marshall a hearing. Apparently, the NAACP counsel spoke convincingly: The day after the meeting, Allred ordered the Texas Rangers to stand guard at the Dallas courthouse, requested an FBI investigation of the incident, and announced that he would tolerate no further harassment of potential black jurors. "No one," observed Richard Kluger, "could remember the last time a southern governor had demonstrated quite as much enthusiasm for enforcement of the law."

In October 1939, NAACP president Walter White created a new branch of the organization. Officially called the NAACP Legal Defense and Educational Fund, Inc., the body would provide free legal aid to blacks who suffered injustice because of their race. According to its charter, the Fund, as it came to be known, would also "seek and promote educational opportunities denied to Negroes because of their color" and publicize reports on "the status of the Negro in American life."

Appointed director-counsel of the Fund, Marshall was responsible for supervising all legal activities for the NAACP; he planned its overall courtroom strategy, oversaw individual lawsuits, prepared briefs, and often argued cases himself. During its early years, the Fund focused on two major targets: racial inequality in the nation's courtrooms and the exclusion of blacks from the voting process.

Marshall prepared his first Supreme Court brief in 1940, when the NAACP sought to overturn the convictions of three black men accused of murdering a white man in Florida. The three had confessed to the crime after a five-day, nonstop grilling by Florida police. During their interrogation, the defendants were not allowed to see lawyers, friends, or family members. The Supreme Court had already ruled that confessions extracted by force could not be used in court, but Florida courts had found that the men's confessions had not been obtained by force and were therefore admissible in court.

In his Supreme Court brief, Marshall maintained that such "sunrise confessions," wrung from terrified and isolated men, qualified as forced admissions. And such confessions, he argued, violated the Fourteenth Amendment's guarantee of "due process of law." Agreeing with Marshall, the Supreme Court reversed the convictions of the three Florida men. The decision in the case, known as *Chambers v. Florida*, by no means eliminated prejudice, violence, and injustice against blacks, but it was an important victory, encouraging to the black community and its defenders.

The next year, Marshall took on another case involving involuntary confessions, this one in Hugo, Oklahoma. After discovering the bodies of Elmer Rogers, his wife, and two children in the smoldering ruins of their home, the police arrested a young black handyman known as Lyons. Although they had no solid evidence against Lyons, police officers held him in a cell for 11 days, denying him food and sleep, beating him severely, and refusing him access to a

A sheriff and his deputies surround a black Oklahoman accused of murdering a white family in 1941. Despite evidence that the suspect, a handyman known as Lyons, had confessed to the crime only after savage beatings, Marshall was unable to prevent his conviction and sentence of life imprisonment.

lawyer. At last, after the officers placed the victims' bloody, charred bones in Lyons's lap, he confessed to the multiple murder. Twelve hours later, he signed a second confession at the state penitentiary.

Convinced that Lyons had been framed for the crime of another, Hugo's black community asked the NAACP to defend him. Marshall took the case himself. When he arrived in the small Oklahoma town, he found it boiling with racial hostility. Local blacks formed a network to protect the NAACP attorney, surrounding him with bodyguards and arranging for him to sleep in a different house each night of his stay.

Despite their precautions, Marshall received an unexpected nighttime visit from a white man. Quickly identifying himself as the murdered woman's father, the visitor said he had come with information. He told Marshall he did not know whether Lyons was guilty, but he did know that the accused man had been treated unfairly. A police official, he said, had showed him a "nigger beater" (a crowbar), boasting that it had been used to "beat a confession out of Lyons." The victim's father offered to testify at Lyons's trial.

Thanks in part to his testimony, the trial judge threw out Lyons's first confession, although he allowed the prosecution to refer to it throughout the trial. Under Marshall's relentless cross-examination, police witnesses admitted to their "bone tactic," and a hotel clerk testified that he heard policemen refer to a "nigger beater." But although Marshall introduced a telling exhibit—a photograph of a beaming police officer standing over the bruised and bleeding Lyons—no policeman would admit to the beatings. The officer pictured with Lyons claimed he could not identify the battered man; all blacks, he said under oath, looked alike to him.

The only evidence that could support a conviction was Lyons's second confession. And this, insisted

Marshall, had been obtained through a form of force: Lyons's terror of being subjected to further violent abuse. The Oklahoma court, however, disregarded Marshall's argument. Finding Lyons guilty of murder, it sentenced him to life imprisonment. Although he had failed to clear his client, Marshall's work was widely considered a victory because the court imposed a life sentence rather than the death penalty.

Believing that the *Chambers v. Florida* precedent applied to the Lyons case, Marshall appealed it to the Supreme Court. Again, he argued that Lyons's conviction had been based on inadmissible evidence—a nonvoluntary admission of guilt—and that he had thus been denied "due process of law." But by a vote of six to three, the justices of the Court decided against Marshall, ruling that Lyons's second confession was not "brought about by the earlier mistreatments." The decision marked Marshall's first defeat in a civil rights case. In the course of his career, he would argue 32 cases before the Supreme Court; 27 of these would be resounding triumphs.

Marshall next moved to the crucial area of voting rights. The Fifteenth Amendment, ratified in 1870, gave black men the right to vote. (Neither black nor white American women could vote until 1920.) But despite the amendment and several laws later enacted to strengthen it, the South's white population had no intention of allowing its black citizens to vote. No more than three percent of eligible blacks voted in the South during the 1930s.

The South employed a number of strategies to keep blacks away from the ballot box. Many states enacted poll taxes, or voting fees, that few blacks—the South's poorest residents—could pay. Other states required each would-be voter to pass a "literacy test"; whites were simply asked to spell their own names, but blacks received long, complicated examinations. Alabama, for example, obliged them to "understand and explain any article of the Consti-

Candidates address a segregated audience at a Marianna, Arkansas, election rally in the 1940s. Such events provided many southern blacks, routinely barred from the polls, with their only connection to the political process.

tution of the United States to the satisfaction of the registrars." The few black citizens who could both pass the literacy test and afford the poll tax still faced intimidation, threats, and violence if they tried to exercise their right to vote.

Still another means—perhaps the most effective—of preventing blacks from voting was the "white primary." In a primary election, usually held a few months before a general election, voters select their party's candidates for office. Because the states of the Deep South were solidly Democratic, the candidates who won the Democratic primary were virtually assured of winning the election that followed. Voters in a primary are required to belong to a political party. But the southern Democrats refused membership to blacks, effectively denying them any voice in the electoral process.

In 1944, Marshall decided to make a frontal assault on the white primary. His battlefield would be Texas; his weapon, a lawsuit brought by black Texan Lonnie E. Smith. When white election judge (supervisor) S. E. Allwright blocked Smith's attempt to vote in the 1940 Texas primary election, Smith sued the Democratic party. His suit was dismissed by the lower courts, which ruled that the Democratic party was a private institution with the right to include—or exclude—whomever it chose.

At this point, Marshall and his Legal Defense Fund team brought the case to the U.S. Supreme Court. They based their principal argument on the Fifteenth Amendment, which forbids the states to deprive citizens of their right to vote "on account of race, color, or previous condition of servitude." Marshall pointed out that the Texas primary "effectively controls the choice" of candidates in the Texas elections. Because the Texas election judge who prevented Smith from voting in the primary was a state official, he argued, the state of Texas had violated the Fifteenth Amendment. "The right to vote in Texas primary elections," he insisted, "is secured by the Constitution."

With only one dissenting vote, the Court upheld the Marshall team's argument, a decision that made racial discrimination in primary elections illegal. Southern states would continue to search for ways to get around the ruling, but in the long run, *Smith v. Allwright* sounded the death knell for the white primary.

Marshall saw the *Smith* decision as both a major triumph in the battle for social justice and as a stepping-stone to future victories. Speaking before an NAACP convention three months later, the exultant attorney asserted that the fight had just begun. "We must not be delayed by people who say, 'the time is not ripe,' " he told a cheering audience. "Persons who deny to us our civil rights should be brought to justice now. Many people believe the time is always 'ripe' to discriminate against Negroes. All right, then—the time is always 'ripe' to bring them to justice."

Not long afterward, Marshall experienced a frightening brush with people who believed the time was "always ripe to discriminate." It occurred near Columbia, Tennessee, on a dark November night in 1946. Earlier in the year, four Columbia policemen had been wounded during a raid on the town's black

A somber banner hangs from the window of the NAACP's New York office. Despite frequent reports of atrocities against blacks (according to police officials, 3,446 black Americans were lynched between 1882 and 1968), most legislators, afraid to incur the enmity of powerful southern politicians, looked the other way.

neighborhood. When 25 black men were subsequently charged with attempted murder, Marshall and 2 staff members sped to Columbia to defend them. After getting 24 of the defendants acquitted, the NAACP lawyers headed for their hotel in Nashville. Suddenly, three patrol cars, sirens wailing, signaled the black attorneys to pull over. Armed constables poured out of the squad cars.

After vainly searching the black lawyers' car for illegal liquor, the constables released Marshall and his friends. But a few miles farther on, they stopped them again. This time, they accused Marshall of drunk driving, ordered him into the squad car, and whisked him back to Columbia. There they told him to get out and walk across the street to the magistrate's office—alone. Aware that many blacks had been given similar orders, only to be shot in the back for allegedly "escaping custody," Marshall refused. The constables then escorted him into the office of the magistrate, a nondrinker famed for his tough approach to drinking drivers. He sniffed Marshall's breath, found him completely sober, and set him free. ("After that," Marshall joked later, "I really *needed* a drink!")

Hoping to avoid further harassment, Marshall's associates had meanwhile traded cars with a local friend. As the NAACP lawyers traveled to Nashville, a carload of deputies followed the friend, dragged him out of the car, and beat him severely. The next day, Marshall wired the U.S. attorney general, demanding a federal investigation of the episode. A week later, he returned to Columbia, strode into the courthouse, and obtained an acquittal for the last of the 25 black defendants.

Morgan v. Virginia, a second Marshall triumph in 1946, involved segregated transportation. Black traveler Irene Morgan, bound for Maryland, had boarded a bus in Virginia. Ordered to sit in the back of the bus as Virginia law dictated, Morgan refused; as an interstate vehicle, she said, the bus was not bound by local law. The driver called the police, who arrested Morgan and fined her $10. Marshall took her case to the Supreme Court, arguing that the Court had already banned state laws that placed "an undue burden" on interstate commerce and that Virginia's bus-passenger segregation law constituted just such a burden.

Concluding his argument, Marshall referred to World War II, which had ended the year before: "Today we are just emerging from a war in which all of the people of the United States were joined in a death struggle against the apostles of racism. How much clearer, therefore, must it be today . . . that the national business of interstate commerce is not to be disfigured by . . . racial notions alien to our national ideals." The Supreme Court agreed with the NAACP attorney, ruling segregation illegal on interstate buses. Although the decision covered only a narrow field, it was a breakthrough that would eventually lead to the end of Jim Crow transportation in America.

The year 1946 also brought Marshall the NAACP's highest award, the Spingarn Medal. Named for longtime NAACP chief Joel Spingarn, the coveted golden award is bestowed each year for the "highest or noblest achievement by an American Negro." A struggling Baltimore attorney only 13 years earlier, Marshall had beaten the odds facing any ambitious young black American in the 1930s. Now one of the nation's best-known lawyers, he had also become one of its most powerful crusaders for social justice. ❧

5

"MR. CIVIL RIGHTS"

B Y THE TIME Thurgood Marshall reached the age of 40, in 1948, he had earned a nickname from the press: "Mr. Civil Rights." Deeply respected by thousands of Americans of all races—and loathed by thousands of others—Marshall remained unchanged in his personal style. Like other associates, Marian Wynn Perry found him as informal and accessible as ever. Perry, a white labor lawyer who worked at the Fund from 1945 until 1949, later talked to Richard Kluger about her boss:

> He had a terribly deep and real affection for the little people—the people he called the Little Joes, and the affection was returned. . . . At a national convention, some little fellow might ask a not very penetrating question and . . . someone else on the rostrum might wave him off. But Thurgood would send me to find the fellow or go see him himself because he knew that question was terribly important to this Little Joe, even if not to anyone else. He had this enormous ability to relate. He was not only *of* them—he was *with* them.

In postwar America, the needs of the "Little Joes" were many. Perhaps most pressing, Marshall and his colleagues believed, was the need for decent housing, especially for the nation's black veterans. Marshall had long complained that the U.S. government itself practiced segregationist housing policies. In 1944, for example, the Federal Housing Administration had built several large public-housing units in Detroit. Addressing an NAACP meeting, Marshall noted that a year after the Detroit project was complete, "every single white family in the area eligible for public

NAACP branch-office director Gloucester Current points out trouble spots to Thurgood Marshall, counsel-director of the NAACP Legal Defense and Educational Fund. Constantly moving from one area of tension to another, Marshall logged thousands of miles of travel each year.

housing had been accommodated and there were still some 800 'white' units vacant with 'no takers.' At the same time there were some 5,000 Negroes inadequately housed and with no units open to them. This is the inevitable result of 'separate but equal' treatment."

Racially integrated American neighborhoods were virtually nonexistent in the 1940s. Blacks were largely confined to ghettos in the cities and to the least desirable sections in smaller towns. Even if a black family could afford a home in a middle- or upper-class neighborhood, no white owner would dream of selling or renting them any property.

Guarding the exclusivity of white neighborhoods were *restrictive covenants*, written agreements between white home buyers and sellers. In signing such an agreement, the buyer agreed never to sell or rent the property to anyone of a different race (or, sometimes, a different religion). In many cities and towns, entire neighborhoods signed restrictive covenants, making all the homes in the district unavailable to blacks. Although a number of prospective black home buyers had taken their cases to court, none had ever succeeded in overturning a restrictive covenant. Nothing in the Constitution, the Supreme Court had ruled in 1926, "prohibits private individuals from entering into contracts respecting . . . their own property."

In early 1947, Marshall and his Legal Defense Fund decided it was time to take action against racially restrictive covenants. Combining three separate anticovenant suits, each of which had lost in the lower courts, the NAACP asked the Supreme Court to consider the issue. Marshall handled *McGhee v. Sipes*, a case involving Orsel McGhee and his wife, blacks who had bought a house in a racially restricted Detroit subdivision. When the next-door neighbors, a white family named Sipes, learned of the purchase, they obtained a court order prohibiting the McGhees from moving into their new home. Michigan's highest court had upheld the ruling against the McGhees.

The Supreme Court took the combined covenant cases, known as *Shelley v. Kraemer*, in the fall of 1947. Lined up on the plaintiffs' side was a formidable array of NAACP legal muscle: Charles Houston, Thurgood Marshall, prominent West Coast attorney Loren Miller, and George Vaughn of St. Louis. Their force was strengthened by support from U.S. attorney general Tom Clark. Responding to Marshall's plea, Clark filed an *amicus curiae* (friend of the court: an individual who is not an actual party in a lawsuit but who has an interest in the matter) brief, urging the court to declare restrictive covenants illegal.

After presenting a long, painstakingly researched brief, Marshall summarized his position to the Court. "This case," he said, "is not a matter of enforcing an isolated private agreement. It is a test as to whether we will have a united nation or a nation divided into areas and ghettoes solely on racial and religious lines." Striking down restrictive covenants, he concluded, would "allow a flexible way of life to develop in which each individual will be able to live, work, and raise his family as a free American."

In May 1948, the Supreme Court handed down its verdict: Restrictive covenants could no longer be enforced by the courts of the land. Marshall and his associates had racked up another victory. Although blacks and other minorities would still face many difficulties in attempting to move into once-restricted neighborhoods, they now had the full weight of the Supreme Court behind them. As one measure of *Shelley*'s impact, 4 years after the decision 21,000 black Chicago families had moved into districts previously closed to them.

Meanwhile, under the leadership of President Harry S. Truman, the federal government was taking major civil rights action. In early 1947, before the

The dilapidated homes in a black Atlanta neighborhood and the Georgia State Capitol (in background) seem to belong to different worlds. In the years following World War II, Marshall and his associates waged a successful campaign against "restrictive covenants," agreements that had long prevented blacks from buying or renting homes in white neighborhoods.

U.S. attorney general entered the *Shelley* case as a "friend," Truman had appointed a prestigious, biracial group of citizens to study America's racial problems. In October 1947, the President's Committee on Civil Rights produced *To Secure These Rights*, a powerful document that called for swift action to end segregation and other abuses of blacks' civil rights. After receiving the committee's report, Truman asked Congress to make lynching a federal offense, to outlaw the poll tax, to eliminate segregated interstate transportation, and to establish a Fair Employment Practices Commission, which would stop racial discrimination in hiring. A year later, Truman ordered an end to all discrimination in federal employment and all segregation in the nation's armed services.

These were giant steps, greeted with jubilation by Marshall and other civil rights crusaders. The achievement of racial justice, however, would require many more steps. Education remained the biggest problem. For the moment, Marshall continued to aim his antisegregation attacks at the nation's graduate schools, reasoning that integration at this level would meet with far less impassioned resistance than integration at the public school level. Expanding on this idea to a friend, Marshall said, "Those racial supremacy boys somehow think that little kids of six or seven are going to get funny ideas about sex and marriage just from going to school together, but for some equally funny reason, youngsters in law school aren't supposed to feel that way. We didn't get it, but we decided if that was what the South believed, then the best thing for the movement was to go along."

Also directing the NAACP counsel's efforts toward graduate schools was the flood of black World War II veterans. Thousands of these former servicemen were not only eager to pursue their education but able to pay for it through the GI Bill, which provided government funds for the schooling of former soldiers. Ambitious black veterans, however, found few educational opportunities open to them, particularly in the South and Southwest. In all the southern states, there was 1 black medical school (but 29 for whites), 1 black law school (but 40 for whites), 1 black pharmacy college (but 20 for whites), and no black engineering school (but 36 for whites.) Clearly, only desegregation of the white institutions could provide the facilities required by black veterans and other black students.

Marshall's first major postwar desegregation battles began in Texas and Oklahoma. Their outcome, technically a victory, would also be a crushing disappointment to the NAACP and its chief counsel. The Texas case revolved around Heman Marion Sweatt, a black letter carrier who applied to the University of Texas Law School in 1946. Academically qualified, Sweatt was rejected because of his race. Texas, however, had no law schools open to blacks.

The U.S. Supreme Court ordered the Universities of Texas and Oklahoma to stop discriminating against Heman Marion Sweatt (right) and George McLaurin (left) after hearing Marshall's arguments. Marshall, who had hoped the McLaurin and Sweatt cases would finally demolish the Plessy v. Ferguson "separate but equal" doctrine, found the Court's narrow decision deeply disappointing.

When Sweatt sued the university, a Texas district judge ruled that the state must either open an "equal" law school within six months or admit Sweatt to its own law school.

Texas responded by slapping together a "colored" law school: two rented rooms for a campus and two black lawyers for faculty. Rejecting this feeble compromise, Sweatt sued again. Texas then opened a new black law school, this one boasting three rented rooms and three part-time instructors. Once again turning down the state's solution, Sweatt went back to court. At this point, Thurgood Marshall appeared on the scene.

Interviewed by a reporter when he arrived in Austin, Texas, Marshall made his intentions clear. "I think we've humored the South long enough," he said, "and it's only by lawsuits and legislation that we'll ever teach reactionaries [extreme conservatives] the meaning of the Fourteenth Amendment. . . . This is going to be a real showdown fight against Jim Crow in education."

Many of the university's students expressed solid support for Sweatt, even opening a temporary, all-white campus branch of the NAACP. The state of Texas, however, planned to defend Jim Crow with all the resources at its command. Marshall brought in a parade of expert witnesses, including the dean of a Pennsylvania law school and a celebrated anthropologist. He also produced an imposing array of statistics and examples to prove that Sweatt could not possibly obtain an equal legal education at the school Texas had opened. Countering Marshall's arguments was future Texas governor Price Daniel, a fervent segregationist and self-described white supremacist. Daniel cross-examined Marshall's witnesses, noted one observer, "as if they were cattle rustlers." The judge made no effort to restrain Daniel's racist remarks, but Marshall remained outwardly cool.

James Nabrit, Marshall's assistant at the Sweatt trial, later talked to Richard Kluger about his colleague. "[Marshall] had the rare ability to know when and where to draw the line in his fervor," said Nabrit. "He was fuming over the judge in Austin, and he said to me before court began one morning, 'I'm gonna tell that judge what I think of him today.' I told him to take it easy. He said nothing in court, but after the case was over and we were all heading for the cars, there was Thurgood standing over in the corner apparently muttering to himself. When he came back to join us, I asked him what that was all about, and he said, 'I told you I was gonna tell that judge what I thought of him—and I just did.' He could do that."

Nevertheless, Marshall lost the case. The Texas Court of Appeals ruled that the state had indeed provided equal opportunities for Sweatt. The NAACP counsel then appealed to the Supreme Court, which agreed to hear the case in due time. Meanwhile, Sweatt went back to delivering mail.

While *Sweatt v. Painter* (Painter was the president of the University of Texas) crept up the Supreme Court's crowded calendar, Marshall took on the Oklahoma graduate school case, which would come to be known as *McLaurin v. Oklahoma State Regents for Higher Education*. George W. McLaurin, a 68-year-old black college professor, had already earned a master's degree; in 1948, he decided to seek a doctorate in education from the University of Oklahoma. Rejected on the basis of his race, he sued. After Marshall convinced an Oklahoma district court that McLaurin could get the education he wanted only at the University of Oklahoma, the court ordered him admitted to the school.

University officials found their own way of coping with this unwelcome integration: They let McLaurin enroll, but "on a segregated basis." The black professor was required to sit outside classroom doors during lectures, given a screened-off desk in the library, and allowed to eat in the school cafeteria only when no white students were dining. Like their Texas counterparts, Oklahoma's white students warmly supported their black classmate, but university officials stood fast. Their treatment of McLaurin, they said, fully complied with Oklahoma's separate-but-equal laws.

Marshall then returned to the district court, arguing that McLaurin's "required isolation from all other students, solely because of the accident of birth, creates a mental discomfiture, which makes concentration and study difficult, if not impossible." The court ruled against him, whereupon he appealed directly to the Supreme Court.

The Supreme Court heard both *Sweatt* and *McLaurin* on the same day in April 1950. By this time, Marshall was determined to do more than try to force states to comply with the "equal" part of "separate but equal." He hoped to prove that, as he had put it in an earlier brief, "the terms 'separate' and 'equal' can not be used conjunctively. . . . *There can be no separate equality.*" Marshall, in short, was aiming at the destruction, once and for all, of the separate-but-equal doctrine, laid down in the *Plessy* decision more than half a century earlier.

Marshall presented his new attack on segregation in his standard tough-minded but nonagressive way, demonstrating respect for his adversaries along with his own unalterable convictions. Explaining his attitude about his opponents, Marshall once remarked to a reporter, "They believe what they believe just as hard as I believe what I believe."

As he waited for the Court's decision on *Sweatt* and *McLaurin*, Marshall must have been thinking of his old mentor and friend, Charles Houston. The battling black attorney, 54 years old, died of a heart attack just after Marshall completed his arguments in the 2 education cases. Marshall, who had learned his craft from the brilliant Houston, probably echoed the sentiments voiced by another old law school colleague, William Hastie, by then a judge of the United States Court of Appeals. "He guided us through the legal wilderness of second-class citizenship," said Hastie of Houston. "He lived to see us close to the promised land of full equality under the law . . . so much closer than would have been possible without his genius and his leadership."

The Supreme Court ruled in favor of both Heman Sweatt and George McLaurin, unanimously but narrowly: Decreeing that Texas had failed to offer Sweatt equal educational opportunity, the Court ordered him admitted to the University of Texas. And ruling that McLaurin's treatment at the University of Oklahoma had served to "impair and inhibit his ability to study," the Court ordered the school to remove its restrictions on the black professor-student. But in neither case did the Court suggest that the *Plessy* doctrine was in

As his mother and his friend Thurgood Marshall look on, young Charles Houston, Jr., accepts the 1950 Spingarn Medal on behalf of his late father, Charles Hamilton Houston. Presenting the coveted NAACP award is Dean Erwin Griswold of the Harvard Law School.

error. Marshall had won the battle, but not the war—at least not yet. Separate but equal remained the law of the land.

Determined to strike down *Plessy*, Marshall plotted his next move, a strategic attack on segregation at the college undergraduate level. One hot, humid night in July 1950, Associated Press reporter Warren Rogers, then stationed in Baton Rouge, Louisiana, received a news tip: Thurgood Marshall and his associates were going to try to enroll 12 black students at Louisiana State University the following day. Marshall, said the tipster, could be found in the back room of a fish-fry parlor in the black district known as Scotlandville.

Recounting the episode in a subsequent article, Rogers said he sped to the dilapidated restaurant. He heard muffled voices as he approached, but they stopped when he knocked on the door. At last, a man spoke from inside: "Who's that?" Rogers identified himself. "What do you want?" asked the man. The journalist said he wanted to talk to Marshall. "What about?" asked the interrogator, whom Rogers now recognized as local NAACP attorney A. P. Tureaud. "About those students you're going to register at LSU tomorrow," responded Rogers. "Another silence," he wrote later. "Somebody sighed. And then a voice, Thurgood Marshall's: 'Let him in.' Introductions all around. But the surliness held until Marshall finally broke it with a loud, thigh-slapping laugh. 'You caught us!' he said. 'Now, we'll talk if you promise not to write anything in advance. We need the surprise, OK?' "

Rogers agreed not to leak the story. The next morning, he watched Tureaud escort 12 nervous but resolute young black people into the admissions office of all-white Louisiana State University. As expected, LSU officials promptly rejected the applications. Just as promptly, Marshall and Tureaud filed suit on behalf

of one of them, a prospective law student named Roy
Wilson. After a district court decided for Wilson,
Marshall asked for, and got, a confirmation from the
Supreme Court of its *Sweatt* decision, a move that
underscored the precedent. Another mile walked,
another 10,000 to go.

In Marshall's case, mileage was more than a figure
of speech. In each of the years since he had joined
the NAACP, he had traveled thousands of miles,
eating irregularly and sleeping when he had time—
rarely more than four hours a night. The grueling
pace had produced marked physical changes. In 1945,
the *Afro-American* had run an illustrated article about
the trim, 6-foot 2-inch, 35-year-old victor of *Smith
v. Allwright*. Accompanying the newspaper's photograph of the movie-star-handsome lawyer was this
comment: "Thurgood Marshall is the amazing type
of man who is liked by other men and probably adored
by women. He carries himself with an inoffensive
self-confidence. . . . He wears and looks especially
well in tweed suits."

The man who succeeded in enrolling a black law
student at LSU in 1950 had lost some of his earlier
sleekness. Marshall no longer had time to worry about
his appearance. His tall frame now carried at least 25
more pounds, and his elegant tweed suits had given
way to rumpled outfits often dusted with cigarette
ashes. *Newsweek* magazine described him as "a di-
sheveled bear of a man," *Time* as "a big, quick-footed
man, with a voice that can be soft or raucous, man-
ners that can be rude or gentle or courtly, and an
emotional pattern that swings him like a pendulum
from the serious to the absurd." To the *New Yorker*,
Marshall was "a tall, vigorous man . . . with a long
face, a long, hooked nose above a black mustache,
and heavy-lidded but very watchful eyes."

Marshall may have stopped being a fashion plate,
but he never slowed down. ("Isn't it nice," he once

jokingly asked, "that no one cares which 23 hours of the day I work?") In 1951, he flew to South Korea for a six-week investigation of alleged mistreatment of black soldiers. American troops had been fighting in the Asian nation since Communist North Korea had invaded its non-Communist neighbor in 1950. An unusually high number of white southern officers commanded the American forces in South Korea, and an unusually high number of black soldiers were being convicted of crimes ranging from "disobedience" to "misbehavior" in battle. When the NAACP started receiving complaints from black soldiers, claiming they had been unjustly treated because of their race, Marshall had decided to take a firsthand look at the situation.

Reviewing military records, interviewing officers and enlisted men, even traveling to the front lines, Marshall examined the cases of 32 black soldiers who had been given heavy sentences. Very few, in his opinion, had received fair hearings. Four men, for example, had received life sentences after trials lasting less than one hour each. Marshall detailed his charges of racism to American commander Douglas MacArthur, but the general gave the attorney no

Black soldiers attack an enemy position at Heartbreak Ridge, site of some of the Korean War's toughest battles. In 1951, Marshall flew to South Korea to investigate charges that the American military was treating black troops unjustly.

assurance that he would take any action. When Marshall arrived back in the United States, therefore, he called a press conference to publicize his findings. Although the army made no official response to Marshall's charges, it soon proved it had heard them: Within weeks, military judges sharply reduced the sentences of 20 of the 32 convicted black soldiers.

Soon after he returned from South Korea, Marshall headed south. His next major case would be *Briggs v. Elliott*, the South Carolina lawsuit pitting Harry Briggs and 19 other black parents against Clarendon County school-board chairman Roderick Elliott. The plaintiffs aimed to force the county to provide their children with schools equal to those it provided white children. Thurgood Marshall and his associates, however, were after bigger game: *Briggs*, they hoped, would be the club with which they could finally kill Jim Crow.

Clarendon County's black citizens had sought at least minimal improvements in their schools for years, but to no avail. Although local white school officials claimed that they offered black students adequate educational facilities, no one could deny the enormous disparities between the county's black and white schools. Provided for the area's 276 white children were 2 brick schoolhouses; 1 teacher for each 28 children; special courses in biology, typing, and bookkeeping; flush toilets; cafeterias; and school buses. The county's 3 black schools, serving 808 pupils, offered a dismal contrast: rickety wooden buildings; 1 teacher for each 47 children; courses in agriculture and home economics; outhouses; no lunchrooms; and no school buses. To reach their assigned schools, black children as young as six had to walk five miles.

At stake in the Briggs case were tremendous issues. If Marshall won, proving not only that Clarendon County's black schools were unequal to its white schools but that they could never be equal

All dressed up for their class picture, a group of young southerners face the camera outside their ramshackle schoolhouse.

unless they were integrated, he could redefine civil rights in America. If he lost, or if he succeeded only in forcing the school board to upgrade the black schools, he would merely have reinforced the separate-but-equal doctrine. Marshall intended to prove that segregation was inherently unequal by proving that it created permanent psychological damage in black children. To strengthen his argument, he had enlisted several expert witnesses. Among them was Dr. Kenneth B. Clark, a 37-year-old assistant professor at City College of New York.

Clark, who would go on to become an eminent sociologist, educator, and author, had made a specialty of studying the effects of segregated schools on black children. With his psychologist wife, Mamie P. Clark, he had designed two tests to measure the attitudes of black children toward race. The tests, which the Clarks had administered to hundreds of young black children in segregated schools, looked simple. In the first test, children were shown four dolls, identical except for their color: Two were brown, two white. Asked which dolls they liked the best and which they considered the "nicest" or the "prettiest," the black children showed "an unmistak-

able preference for the white doll and a rejection of the brown doll," reported the Clarks.

The second test involved crayons and outline drawings of girls and boys. The Clarks found that when black children in segregated schools were asked to color figures representing themselves, a surprising number chose white or pink crayons. To the Clarks and other sociologists, these results showed that black children who received segregated, inferior educations came to feel inferior themselves.

Black people from all over eastern South Carolina poured into Charleston for the *Briggs* trial. By the time the courthouse doors opened at 7:00 A.M. on May 28, 1951, more than 500 people had formed an orderly line from the street to the second-floor court-room. Only 150 spectators could be seated inside the courtroom, but during the trial those inside whispered news of developments to the people outside; they in turn relayed it to their neighbors, until it finally reached the crowds in the street.

Briggs commanded the attention of South Carolina's white as well as its black population. The state's ruling white establishment realized that losing this case could mean losing the way of life it had carefully guarded ever since the Civil War. Attorney Robert Figg, representing the Clarendon County School Board, decided the best defense was an up-front admission that the county's black schools were indeed inferior to its white schools, followed by a promise to upgrade the black schools. In light of the county's position, said Figg, testimony on the inadequate facilities then available to blacks was irrelevant.

Marshall quickly asserted that this unexpected move had no bearing on the case. His aim, he told the court, was to prove the state's segregation laws unconstitutional. In order to do that, he insisted, his side "must be able to show the inequalities as they actually exist." Nevertheless, despite a parade of witnesses confirming the wretchedness of the county's black schools, despite the carefully delivered research of Kenneth Clark and other experts, despite Marshall's powerful arguments, he lost the case.

The court ruled that as long as all students received equal education, segregation could not be proven unconstitutional. Clarendon County's attorneys asserted that the school board would upgrade facilities for blacks within "a reasonable time." Leaving the Charleston courthouse after a subsequent hearing, Marshall was approached by a local attorney. "If you show your black ass in Clarendon County ever again," said the southern lawyer, "you're a dead man." Unimpressed—it was neither the first nor the last such threat he would hear—Marshall gathered his papers and strode from the courtroom.

As soon as the judge ruled on *Briggs*, Marshall made his next move: He appealed the decision to the United States Supreme Court. Meanwhile, he began to receive criticism from some sectors of the black community. In July 1951, the *Courier*, America's largest black newspaper, called *Briggs* "a serious legal setback in the civil rights fight." Marshall's frontal assault on segregation, said the newspaper, had "involved risk where none was necessary," producing a

Parents and children of Virginia's Prince Edward County, plaintiffs in one of the five lawsuits that comprised Brown v. Board of Education, *assemble on the steps of Virginia's State Capitol building in Richmond. The Prince Edward case was a class action, a suit brought by one or more individuals on behalf of an entire group—in this case, all the black schoolchildren of the county.*

decision that "infuses new vigor in the . . . doctrine of 'separate but equal.' "

"All our cases have involved risks," Marshall retorted. "It is completely unrealistic to believe the South will voluntarily . . . equalize school facilities," he replied in the *Courier.* "If we had not threatened to challenge the legality of the segregation system and if we do not continue the challenge to segregated schools, we will get the same thing we have been getting all these years—separate but never equal." Marshall's response drew the backing of black leaders across the nation. "We want our rights now, not a century hence," wrote one prominent black official.

After a series of delays and legal maneuvers, the Supreme Court finally agreed to hear *Briggs,* along with four NAACP segregation suits from Delaware, Kansas, Virginia, and the District of Columbia. Titled *Brown v. Board of Education of Topeka,* the consolidated appeals went before the court on December 9, 1952. After three days of intense oral arguments, both sides had used up the time allotted to them, and the Supreme Court justices retired to consider what they had heard. On his way out of the courtroom, Marshall's opponent, attorney John W. Davis, spoke to a colleague. "I think we've got it won," he said.

The following June, the Court announced that it wanted both Marshall and Davis to clarify certain constitutional points in their arguments. Their next appearance was scheduled for December 7, 1953. Marshall and his colleagues believed that the Court's questions justified optimism. But Marshall refused to be lulled into a sense of false security. The Court's request for clarification, he said, might even "turn out to be a booby trap with a bomb in it." He and his staff set to work with renewed vigor. To help him plan his strategy, Marshall convened a conference of 85 prominent sociologists, historians, political scientists, constitutional experts, and educators.

After grueling months of what one participant called "brain picking," Marshall wrote his brief for the Supreme Court showdown. Its main emphasis was on the Fourteenth Amendment and the intentions of those who had written it. "There can be no doubt," said Marshall, "that the framers were seeking to secure and to protect the Negro as a full and equal citizen." Earlier Supreme Court decisions, he continued, "compel the conclusion that school segregation . . . is at war with the Amendment's intent."

Listening intently to the measured rhetoric on that fateful morning were three of Marshall's closest associates: his old friend and early supporter, Carl Murphy of the *Afro-American*; his mother, Norma Marshall; and his wife and best friend, Vivian "Buster" Marshall.

John W. Davis countered Marshall's argument by asserting that the amendment's authors "did not contemplate and did not understand that it would abolish segregation in public schools." Marshall's case, he said, was nothing more than an effort to prove that black children would be happier or would become better students in integrated schools. And, he added, Marshall had not even proved *that*. The justices of the Supreme Court thought otherwise. Five months later, they unanimously declared school segregation unconstitutional.

For Thurgood Marshall, the decision crowned half a lifetime of dedicated labor. He later described his reaction to the news: "I was so happy I was numb." His happiness, however, was soon shadowed by sorrow. Shortly after the decision, Buster Marshall told her husband she was dying of cancer. Although she had known of her condition for months, she had kept it to herself, refusing to let it interfere with her husband's concentration on the most important case he would ever argue. When Marshall learned of his wife's fatal illness, he nearly collapsed. For 25 years, Buster Marshall had been not only his wife but his closest ally.

During the following fall and winter, Thurgood Marshall spent every available minute with his wife, and in the last six weeks of her life, he remained at her bedside constantly. Buster Marshall died in February 1955. "I thought the end of the world had come," Thurgood Marshall said afterward.

Most Americans believed the end of segregated schools had come with the 1954 *Brown* decision, but Jim Crow would not disappear so easily. Five weeks after Chief Justice Warren read the opinion, the governor of Virginia said, "I shall use every legal means at my command to continue segregated schools in Virginia." Similar responses echoed through much of the South. The governor of Georgia said the decision had turned the Constitution into "a mere scrap of paper." North Carolina's governor said he was "terribly disappointed." South Carolina's governor said he was "shocked."

Not all southerners, however, reacted negatively. Speaking for the region's many moderates, University of North Carolina scholar Howard Odum said, "The South is likely to surprise itself and the nation and do an excellent job of readjustment. We might want to delay a little so we can get ready, but in my opinion, the South for the most part will take it in stride."

Attending a racially mixed class for the first time in their lives, two Virginia schoolgirls exchange curious glances at a Fort Myer elementary school on September 8, 1954. The date, four months after the U.S. Supreme Court declared segregation unconstitutional, marked the beginning of integrated public schooling in Virginia.

Thurgood Marshall predicted that by 1963, the 100th anniversary of the Emancipation Proclamation, American school segregation would be history.

The *Brown* decision declared school segregation unconstitutional, but it did not say when it had to take effect. After its May 1954 decision, the Supreme Court heard months of testimony from southern spokesmen and from Marshall and his staff. The South, predictably, wanted as long a time period as it could get; the NAACP, predictably, wanted desegregation to begin at once. Finally, in May 1955, the Court delivered its decision on putting *Brown* into practice.

The states, said the Court, were required to admit to their public schools all eligible sudents "on a racially nondiscriminatory basis with all deliberate speed." Noting that "public interest" in some areas would make desegregation difficult, the Court allowed states to take whatever time was "necessary" to complete their desegregation plans, as long as they demonstrated "good faith." Thus, in spite of Marshall's passionate plea for a fixed date for the completion of desegregation, the segregationist states gained time to practice the strategy of delay. *Brown II*, as the 1955 decision came to be called, was a heavy blow to Marshall and his team. Full and immediate justice for America's black children, seemingly within reach a year earlier, had once more become a long-term goal.

Still, thanks to both *Brown* decisions, desegregation was on its way. Thurgood Marshall considered the situation, weighed his alternatives, and decided he had more than enough reason to hope. Soon after *Brown II* came down, he telephoned his friend Carl Murphy at the *Afro-American*. (Taped by Murphy's office, the dialogue was quoted by Richard Kluger in *Simple Justice*.) State laws mandating segregation, said Marshall, "have got to yield. They've got to yield to the Constitution. And yield means yield! Yield means give up!"

Murphy asked Marshall what he planned to do.

"We're going to do state by state, that's what we hope," responded the NAACP counsel. "For example, we're going to treat Georgia one way, we're going to treat Maryland another way. But now if Maryland doesn't act right, then we treat Maryland like we treat Georgia. . . . And we're going to give West Virginia a chance. Virginia we're going to bust wide open! . . . You can say all you want but those white crackers are going to get tired of having Negro lawyers beating 'em every day in court."

In a more solemn mode, Marshall addressed a Howard University forum. "The Negro who was once enslaved by law became emancipated by it, and is achieving equality through it. . . . I think *Brown v. Board of Education* demonstrates [that law] can also change social patterns. Provided it is adequately enforced, law can change things for the better; moreover, it can change the hearts of men, for law has an educational function also." ✺

6

"A LONG, RESPECTFUL WHISTLE"

THE *BROWN* DECISIONS provided Thurgood Marshall with both deep satisfaction and additional professional stress. New developments in his private life, however, helped ease the burden. In late 1955, the 47-year-old Marshall began courting Hawaiian-born Cecilia Suyat, an NAACP secretary known to her friends as Cissy. Colleagues saw the quiet, even-tempered Suyat and the boisterous, dynamic Marshall as perfect foils for each other. The couple apparently agreed: They married in December 1955.

A few months later, in February 1956, Marshall called a meeting of southern civil rights lawyers in Atlanta, Georgia. After hearing reports on local progress (or lack of it) in school integration, he called for ongoing pressure on a case-by-case basis. The lawsuits that followed inspired not only complex legal maneuvering but hostility, boycotts, and, sometimes, rioting that required armed intervention.

By far, the most violent resistance to integration took place in Little Rock, Arkansas. The Little Rock school board had prepared to admit black students to the city's Central High School in the fall of 1957 and to follow up with the desegregation of junior high and elementary schools. But Arkansas governor Orval Faubus had other ideas. A staunch segregationist, Faubus dispatched Arkansas National Guard units to Central High, ordering them to prevent the entrance

Trailed by photographers and reporters, Marshall and his wife, the former Cecilia (Cissy) Suyat, leave the U.S. Supreme Court after a hearing in the mid-1950s. The couple, who married in late 1955, met at the NAACP's New York office, where Suyat worked as a legal secretary.

of the nine black students who had registered there. The school board then petitioned the local district judge, who ordered the integration plan carried out immediately.

Faubus defied the court order, keeping the guardsmen at the school doors and blocking the black students' entry. For the next three weeks, the students arrived at the school every morning, greeted not only by armed soldiers but by a mob of white adults screaming racist epithets and threatening the teenagers with physical harm.

At this point, Thurgood Marshall stepped in. As counsel for the black students, he obtained another court order, this one forbidding Faubus or the national guard to interfere with the desegregation of Central High School. Not even that worked. No less an official than the president of the United States, Dwight D. Eisenhower, was required to maintain order in Little Rock. Eisenhower sent the 327th Battle Group of the 101st Airborne Division to Central High, and black students finally gained admittance. Racial tension in Little Rock remained sharp, how-

Marshall shares a laugh with colleagues at a 1955 meeting of civil rights lawyers in Atlanta, Georgia. Famed for his steely determination to obtain legal and social justice for blacks, Marshall has also gained renown for his hilarious—and occasionally mildly shocking—jokes and anecdotes.

Followed by a crowd of support-ive Alabamans, Marshall strides through the streets of Birmingham in February 1956. The NAACP counsel was escorting Autherine Lucy (front row, left) to district court, where he later obtained an order forcing the University of Alabama to admit the 26-year-old black woman as a student.

ever, and in June the school board asked the district court to let it postpone desegregation for two and a half years.

Under Marshall's direction, the case eventually reached the Supreme Court. When Marshall addressed the Court in September 1958, he asserted that local resistance had no place in determining the law of the land. Even if desegregation produces unrest, he said, "this is preferable to the complete breakdown of education which will result from teaching that courts of law will bow to violence." The case, he added, gave the Court the chance to affirm "the supremacy of all constitutional rights over bigots—big and small."

The Court ruled in Marshall's favor. Still unwilling to give up, Faubus ordered the state's racially mixed public schools closed. Once again, Marshall appealed to the Supreme Court, which declared Faubus's action unconstitutional. Finally, by fall 1959, Little Rock's black and white children began their school year together and in peace.

During the next few years, Marshall engaged in seemingly unending legal combat, defending integration in Louisiana, Alabama, Virginia, South Carolina, and Texas. Alabama even tried to ban the NAACP from operating in the state, a move that brought Marshall back to the Supreme Court. "The right of freedom of association and free speech," he argued, belongs to "unpopular minorities" as well as to groups approved by "those in power." The safeguarding of these freedoms, he added, indicated "a belief in the fundamental good sense of the American people." The Alabama suit against the NAACP dragged on for five years, bouncing back and forth between the Supreme Court and the Alabama courts; but in the end, Marshall won: The NAACP continued to operate in Alabama.

In addition to waging a nonstop campaign against school segregation, Marshall and his Legal Defense Fund fought dozens of battles for individual rights. In 1961, for example, they took the case of Charles Clarence Hamilton, a black citizen of Alabama who had been convicted of raping a white woman and sentenced to death. Because Hamilton had not been advised of his rights or given legal counsel, Marshall argued, he had been deprived of "due process of law." Once again accepting a Marshall argument, the Supreme Court reversed Hamilton's conviction.

Marshall's attack points also included public housing, recreational facilities, interstate and local buses and trains, and professional sports arenas. He and his colleagues won blacks the right to use state-supported beaches in Maryland, to live in municipal housing in Missouri, to play on public golf courses in Georgia, to eat in railroad station restaurants in Virgina, to compete in boxing matches in Louisiana, and to sit at the front of buses in South Carolina.

The bus seat issue had become national news in 1955 when Rosa Parks, a 43-year-old black seamstress in Montgomery, Alabama, refused to give up her bus seat to a white passenger. Parks's arrest led to a black boycott of Montgomery's buses that lasted for more than a year. Organizing the boycott was Martin Luther King, Jr., a 26-year-old black Montgomery clergyman who soon became one of the 20th century's most influential black leaders.

King's struggle in Montgomery had the full support of Marshall and his Legal Defense Fund. In 1956, when King's advisers asked Marshall if he would back the Montgomery boycott—which eventually succeeded in desegregating the city's buses—the NAACP counsel guaranteed the legal protection of the Montgomery Improvement Association, the organization formed by King and other black leaders to direct the boycott. Marshall must have applauded King's words, spoken after his arrest during the bus boycott: "One thing the gradualists don't seem to understand: We are not trying to make people love us when we go to court; we are trying to keep them from killing us."

As the nation entered the 1960s, concerned Americans staged increasingly frequent, nonviolent protests against racial discrimination. Black southerners silently knelt on the steps of white churches, sat at "whites only" restaurant counters, and occupied train and bus seats traditionally reserved for whites. But even after the triumph in Montgomery, civil rights demonstrators faced harassment and arrest throughout the South. In 1960, Marshall publicly committed "the whole force of the NAACP" to defending civil rights demonstrators. "If a store is open to the public, anyone who enters is entitled to the same service anyone else gets," he said. "The right of protest is part of our tradition. It goes back to tea dumped in Boston Harbor. They have a right to say they want their rights. As long as they act lawfully, we will support them."

Marshall soon proved he meant what he said. The following year, police in Baton Rouge, Louisiana, arrested 16 black students for refusing to leave a segregated lunch counter. Although the neatly dressed

Marshall and NAACP attorney W. J. Durham lay plans to thwart the Dallas school board's 1959 request for a delay in integration. When one local segregationist said that the different educational levels of black and white children made integration a problem, Marshall replied, "Put the dumb colored children in with the dumb white children, and put the smart colored children with the smart white children—that is no problem."

students had remained silent during their sit-in, they had been booked for "disturbing the peace," a time-honored southern charge against unwelcome blacks. Found guilty in the Louisiana courts, each of the students received a $100 fine and a 30-day jail sentence. Thurgood Marshall took their case, known as *Garner v. Louisiana*, to the Supreme Court. He argued that the demonstrators' arrest, "based upon a vague statute which is enforced by the police according to their personal notions," violated their rights to both due process of law and freedom of expression. For the 29th time, the justices of the Supreme Court agreed with Marshall. They unanimously reversed the convictions of all 16 defendants, a victory that impressed even die-hard segregationists. The black attorney, grudgingly admitted Senator Richard B. Russell of Georgia, seemed to wield "an almost occult power" over the United States Supreme Court.

Garner v. Louisiana marked Marshall's last appearance as NAACP chief counsel. Although he remained passionately committed to the organization he had served for 27 years, he hoped it could disappear one day. In the early 1960s, a reporter asked him to define the NAACP's ultimate purpose. "To go out

Angry white youths, some of them carrying chains and hammers, accost black demonstrators after a Portsmouth, Virginia, lunch counter sit-in. Such confrontations became increasingly frequent during the 1960s, a decade of massive social change in the United States.

of business," replied Marshall, "with a realization that race is no longer a problem."

That realization, of course, lay far in the future. Meanwhile, Marshall had more work to do. In September 1961, 8 months after John F. Kennedy took office as the 35th president of the United States, he nominated Thurgood Marshall for a judgeship on the Court of Appeals for the Second Circuit.

The federal judicial system is made up of three tiers. At the lowest level are the district courts, where federal cases are tried and decisions rendered. If the losing party in a lawsuit is dissatisfied with the ruling of a district court, that party can appeal to the next highest tribunal, a circuit court of appeals. Appeals court decisions are final unless they are reviewed and overturned by the U.S. Supreme Court. A litigant dissatisfied with a circuit court decision may appeal to the Supreme Court, but most litigants' chances of being heard are slight. The Supreme Court receives about 5,000 requests for appeal every year—many more than it can handle—and it turns most of them down. The Court hears only about 200 cases, generally those that raise important constitutional issues, each year.

Each of the 11 circuits (geographic regions) within the federal court system has its own court of appeals. The Second Circuit Court of Appeals serves the states of New York, Vermont, and Connecticut. Because the Second Circuit decides an unusually high number of important cases, the legal world regards appointment to its bench as a high honor. Delighted by the president's recognition of their hero, civil rights advocates greeted Marshall's nomination with cheers. But there was no joy among white conservatives, none of whom wanted to see a liberal black lawyer on the federal bench.

Before they can be seated, nominees for federal judgeships must gain the approval of the Senate Ju-

Democratic senator James O. Eastland of Mississippi led the conservatives' 1961 fight against Marshall's confirmation as a federal judge. Deeply resentful of Marshall's success as a civil rights champion, Eastland first ignored the nominee, then hazed him, then said his background was inappropriate for a circuit judge, and finally suggested he was linked with "radical elements." Despite Eastland's attacks, the Senate confirmed Marshall's nomination.

diciary Committee. In 1961, the committee's members included its chairman, Mississippi's ultraconservative James O. Eastland, several other southern Democrats, and a few conservative Republicans. They subjected Marshall to a trial by fire, cross-examining him ferociously and dragging out his confirmation hearings for almost a year. Unflappable as always, Marshall sailed through the ordeal without impatience or apparent loss of temper.

Many senators, including Republican Kenneth B. Keating of New York, found the committee's tactics appalling. Marshall "has helped shape some of the most important legal advances of the decade in the field of civil rights," said Keating. "I propose that his selection be acted upon immediately, for our nation is not so rich in brilliance and talent that we can afford to pigeonhole it, as is being done in the case of Thurgood Marshall."

The Senate Judiciary Committee finally approved Marshall's nomination by a narrow margin. The full Senate then quickly confirmed him by a 54–16 vote. (The 16 nay votes were all cast by southern Democrats.) Senator Phillip A. Hart, a staunch Marshall supporter, probably spoke for many of his colleagues when he reacted to Marshall's victory. "Amen," he said, "and thank heaven."

Marshall took his seat on the federal bench in September 1962. He soon discovered that a judge and an attorney see a courtroom from very different perspectives. Accustomed to working with a battalion of noisy, impassioned lawyers in the always busy, sometimes frantic atmosphere of civil rights law, he now found himself in an isolated, somber environment.

Marshall's former secretary later told a *Life* magazine reporter that her boss "never complained about the court. In fact, he said he liked it." However, said the secretary, Marshall occasionally seemed lonely.

Chief Appeals Court judge J. Edward Lumbard swears Marshall in as a federal judge in 1961. To the surprise—and dismay—of those who had opposed his confirmation, Marshall chalked up an impressive record during his four years on the Second Circuit: Not one of his 98 majority opinions was ever reversed by the U.S. Supreme Court.

"Often his only visitor would be the bailiff," she said. "The other justices kept their chamber doors closed, but he insisted his be kept open."

During his 4-year tenure on the Second Circuit Court of Appeals, Marshall and his fellow justices decided some 400 cases each year. Marshall himself wrote 118 majority and dissenting opinions, many of them relating to cases totally unlike those he had spent his life practicing. He ruled on such issues as maritime law, patents and trademarks, and labor relations. One of his most admired opinions, however, dealt with familiar grounds: the First Amendment's guarantee of freedom of expression.

In 1965, the University of the State of New York ordered its faculty members to sign loyalty oaths, swearing that they had never been affiliated with the Communist party. The signing of loyalty oaths had become an important issue in the United States, stirring heated controversy between conservatives, who approved of the oaths, and liberals, who called them unconstitutional. Any faculty member who failed to sign the oath, said New York's university officials,

Marshall regales a group of dignitaries at a ceremony marking the Emancipation Proclamation's 100th anniversary. With the circuit court judge are Governor Nelson Rockefeller of New York (left), and UN ambassador Adlai Stevenson.

faced immediate dismissal. The university based its demand on the Feinberg Law, a state regulation that permitted the dismissal of public school teachers who refused to sign such oaths.

Believing that the law violated the Fourteenth Amendment's "due process" clause, faculty member Harry Keyishian and several colleagues sued the university in district court. The district court refused to hear the case, asserting that the educators had posed no substantial constitutional question. The faculty members then appealed to the Second Circuit Court.

Marshall, who delivered the court's opinion, ruled that the case, *Keyishian v. Board of Regents of the University of the State of New York*, did raise constitutional questions. He pointed out that the Supreme Court had specifically refused to pass on the constitutionality of laws that required school employees to swear they had never been Communists. In any case, said Marshall, the Feinberg Law applied to public school teachers, not to university faculty members. He also firmly noted that Feinberg had "significant similarity" to other laws that the Supreme Court had recently ruled unconstitutional.

Marshall sent *Keyishian* back to the district court, instructing it to hear the case. When the lower court accordingly reviewed *Keyishian*, it ruled the loyalty oaths constitutional. Two years later, however, the case went to the Supreme Court, which reversed the lower court's decision. Emphatically confirming Marshall's opinion, the Supreme Court held that the Feinberg Law indeed violated the Fourteenth Amendment.

Among circuit judge Marshall's most highly publicized opinions was one dealing with a man who had been tried three times on the same first-degree murder charge. Marshall insisted that states as well as the federal government were obliged to protect accused persons against "double jeopardy." (According to the

Fifth Amendment, "Nor shall any person be subject for the same offense to be twice put in jeopardy of life or limb.") Maintaining that this was exactly what New York State had done to the defendant, Marshall reversed the man's conviction.

"It was a difficult case," observed *New York Times* reporter Sidney Zion in 1965. "But few judges would have bothered to write a 42-page opinion, as he did. . . . It was advocacy at its purest and at the end, agree or not, one could only offer a long, respectful whistle. There wasn't a point that Marshall hadn't dealt with and then with great clarity in prose that could be understood by any intelligent layman. Judges do not usually do this. The general rule is to slide over the high, hard ones." Marshall, added Zion, "seems incapable of dodging the tough questions."

During his years as a federal judge, Marshall ruled on a wide variety of cases; their subjects ranged from the rights of defendants to the deportation of aliens to the use of illegally obtained evidence in criminal trials. In 4 years, not one of Marshall's 98 majority opinions was reversed by the Supreme Court, a remarkable record for a circuit court judge. That record did not go unnoticed in the corridors of power.

One day in July 1965, Marshall was having lunch with his colleagues in New York City when an aide arrived with a message. "The president is on the phone," said the aide. "The president of what?" asked Marshall. "Of the United States, sir," answered the aide. Marshall picked up the telephone and spoke to Lyndon B. Johnson. The president invited the judge to come to Washington, D.C., to talk about a new job: United States solicitor general, the third highest legal position—after attorney general and assistant attorney general—in the land. Marshall went to Washington.

7

SOLICITOR GENERAL

W HEN THURGOOD MARSHALL arrived at the White House in July 1965, President Lyndon Johnson formally asked him to accept the nomination to the post of U.S. solicitor general. "I want folks to walk down the hall at the Justice Department," Johnson reportedly told Marshall, "and see a [black man] sitting there." As solicitor general, Marshall—the first black citizen to hold the post—would be the nation's top-ranking courtroom advocate. On the other hand, taking the position would mean a cut in salary, from $33,000 per year to $28,500. It would also mean giving up a lifetime federal judgeship for an executive post held "at the pleasure of the president."

Marshall accepted the president's offer without skipping a beat. Reporters later asked him why he had made a "sacrifice," taking a position that provided less money and no security. "Because," he said, "the president asked me to." Then he added, "I believe that in this time, especially, we do what our government requests of us. Negroes have made great advances in government and I think it's time they started making some sacrifices."

Looking on as Marshall takes his oath of office as U.S. solicitor general are his wife, Cissy; President Lyndon Johnson; and (far right) U.S. attorney general Nicholas Katzenbach. After the ceremony, Johnson said it would be good for "schoolchildren to know that when the great United States government spoke in the highest court in the land, it did so through a Negro."

The U.S. solicitor general, probably the most publicly visible member of the Justice Department, represents the United States before the Supreme Court. This official directs all cases in which the United States government has an interest and argues the most important cases personally. The solicitor general also decides which cases the Justice Department will ask the Supreme Court to review and what position the department should take on cases being heard by the Court.

Because the president wanted Marshall confirmed as soon as possible, confirmation hearings were scheduled for July 29, only two weeks after the nomination was announced. Marshall took a small apartment in Washington, temporarily leaving his family in New York City. That family by now included not only his wife, Cissy, but two sons, nine-year-old Thurgood, Jr., and John William, seven. After his nomination, Marshall found himself besieged by reporters' questions about his professional and personal life.

One journalist, drawing on widespread rumors about Marshall, asked him how he found time to play poker and watch western movies. Marshall roared with laughter. "Now isn't that something else?" he said. "My newspaper friends keep saying all those things, and I wish to hell it was up to date. Once in a while I'll catch a western on television . . . and poker! Hah! I haven't pushed a chip in 10 years. You know what cards I'm down to now? I play 'War' with my two boys. Now that's hot action for you, isn't it?"

Reporters who interviewed Marshall's colleagues heard the same terms over and over: "natural advocate" and "warm human being." One NAACP lawyer told reporter Sidney Zion that "Thurgood is as comfortable at the Hogwash Junction function as he is at the home of a Supreme Court justice. He relates to everybody and anybody and it's this more than anything else that sets him apart from all the rest."

The hearings on Marshall's nomination as solicitor general contrasted sharply with those he had endured four years earlier. This time, the Senate Judiciary subcommittee approved Marshall's candidacy in exactly 29 minutes; the following day, the full Senate confirmed him with no debate. Thirteen days later, on August 11, Marshall was sworn in by Supreme Court associate justice Hugo Black. "He has good policy judgment and the power of self-control," Black commented afterward. "I know he will do a fine job."

For his swearing-in ceremony, Marshall wore the traditional outfit of the solicitor general: a cutaway morning coat, striped trousers, and a gray vest. "Now isn't this the silliest get-up in the world?" he asked with a broad smile. A reporter asked if he had considered skipping the formal attire. "No, no, I'm too old to worry about changing all that now," the 57-year-old Marshall replied, chuckling. "Besides, I've got a cutaway. . . . Now if I had to go out and buy a new one maybe I'd think about changing the tradition."

Marshall carried his informal manner into the solicitor general's office. During his first week on the job, for example, he burst into an aide's office. "How the hell do you work that noise box in my office?" he roared. "I can't get the World Series anywhere!" But Marshall confined his lighthearted moments to backstage. In the courtroom, he projected the measured dignity observers had come to expect. Between 1965 and 1967, he won 14 of the 19 cases he argued for the United States government. Most of them dealt with civil rights and privacy issues.

One of the major civil rights cases began in Philadelphia, Mississippi. It involved James Chaney, a 21-year-old black Mississippian, and 2 white New Yorkers: Andrew Goodman, 20, and Michael Schwerner, 24. In Mississippi to help register black

Following an official welcome from the U.S. Supreme Court, newly installed solicitor general Marshall leaves the Court with U.S. attorney general Nicholas Katzenbach. Speaking to a reporter after the formal ceremony, Marshall pointed to his attire and said, "Now isn't this the silliest get-up in the world?"

voters—an extremely unpopular and dangerous activity in the South of the early 1960s—the three civil rights workers disappeared in June 1964. After a massive search, FBI agents uncovered the young men's bodies beneath an earthen dam; all had been shot to death. The FBI arrested the local sheriff, his deputy, a patrolman, and 18 others, most of them members of the Ku Klux Klan.

Because murders are prosecuted on a state rather than on a federal level, the United States government may not bring murder charges, no matter how strong its case. In this instance, the Justice Department accused the Mississippi lawmen and Klan members of interfering with the civil rights of citizens—a federal crime. When the local district court dismissed the charges against all but three of the accused men, United States solicitor general Thurgood Marshall moved in. Marshall appealed the district court's ruling to the Supreme Court, requesting reinstatement of charges against all the accused men.

Unanimously agreeing with Marshall's arguments, the Court ordered the accused to stand trial. In the end, an all-white Mississippi jury found 7 of the defendants guilty; each received the maximum sentence of 3 to 10 years in jail. Although the rest were acquitted, Marshall and his staff celebrated the trial's historic outcome: It marked the first occasion that a white southern jury had convicted white defendants in a civil rights case. Civil rights history was on the march.

Marshall owed a number of his triumphs as solicitor general to the Civil Rights Act of 1964—which, in turn, owed its existence to the work of Martin Luther King, Jr., Marshall, and other crusaders for social justice. Among its several provisions, the Civil Rights Act outlawed discrimination in public accommodations—including hotels, theaters, restaurants, parks, and swimming pools—and empowered the Justice Department to bring suits against violators. In 1966, Marshall made use of the Civil Rights Act when he argued *Evans v. Newton*, a case that centered on a semipublic park in Macon, Georgia.

The Macon park had been left to the city by a wealthy resident who directed that it be used only by whites. After the enactment of the Civil Rights Act in 1964, Macon officials opened the park to blacks; as a public facility, they said, it could no longer be legally segregated. The landowner's heirs and other local whites challenged the city's action and won. The city then appealed to the Georgia State Supreme Court, which upheld the challengers.

When the United States Supreme Court agreed to hear the case, Marshall acted as amicus curiae. Although the park was technically private, he argued, it performed a "public function" and therefore came under the provisions of the Civil Rights Act. Writing for the majority of the Court, Associate Justice Wil-

The Reverend Martin Luther King, Jr., displays photographs of (left to right) Michael Schwerner, James Chaney, and Andrew Goodman, the civil rights workers murdered near Philadelphia, Mississippi, in 1964. After hearing Marshall's arguments, the U.S. Supreme Court ordered the young men's accused killers to stand trial in Mississippi, where they were eventually convicted of civil rights violations and sentenced to jail terms.

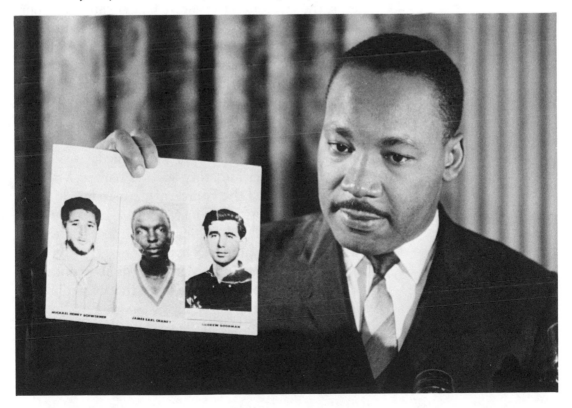

liam O. Douglas responded to Marshall's argument. "Under the circumstances of this case," he said, "we cannot but conclude that the public character of the park requires that it be treated as a public institution." After the decision, Macon's park once more served residents of all races.

Another important Marshall case centered on tenants' rights. In 1964, the California legislature repealed the state's fair housing statutes—laws that prohibited landlords from practicing racial discrimination. When a black couple, the Mulkeys, were refused an apartment by white landlords, the Reitmans, the Mulkeys sued and won in the California courts. Asserting that the California legislature had legalized discrimination, the Reitmans appealed to the United States Supreme Court, which heard the case in 1967.

Marshall argued that, in repealing fair housing laws, the California legislature had violated the Fourteenth Amendment's equal protection clause. According to the Constitution of the United States, he said, the Mulkeys were entitled to live in any apartment they could afford. After listening to Marshall, the Supreme Court ruled that California had illegally taken action "designed to make private discrimination legally possible." The state's constitutional amendment, said the Court, had made it a guilty partner in a discriminatory act and had, as Marshall asserted, violated the Fourteenth Amendment. Marshall had won his case. The Mulkeys—and thousands of other black families—had won the right to live wherever they wanted to live.

As solicitor general, Marshall was also concerned with voting rights. Representing the United States in a 1965 challenge brought by South Carolina, he successfully defended the federal government's right to oversee elections in areas where discrimination had been clearly practiced. In 1966, he secured the right

Solicitor General Marshall discusses a legal point with one of his longtime admirers, Senator Robert Kennedy of New York. As attorney general from 1961 to 1964, Kennedy had strongly supported the black struggle for civil rights, entering school-desegregation cases on the side of black petitioners, encouraging efforts to register black voters in the South, and filing dozens of cases against communities and individuals suspected of infringing on blacks' voting rights.

of non-English-speaking citizens to vote. That year, he also scored a major victory against the poll tax, the Deep South's favorite method of depriving impoverished blacks of their right to vote.

Although the Constitution's Twenty-fourth Amendment (ratified in 1964) prohibited the use of poll taxes in national elections, the issue of poll taxes in local and state elections remained unresolved. Five southern states, including Virginia, continued to require citizens to pay a fee before they cast their state ballots. In 1966, several black Virginians brought suit against the state and its poll taxes. The district court ruled against them, holding that the states, not the federal government, had the right to set voting requirements in state elections.

When the Supreme Court heard the Virginians' appeal, *Harper v. Virginia Board of Elections*, Marshall argued the case on behalf of the United States. The authority of the states to establish voters' qualifications, he maintained, did not extend to the "unbridled license to exclude any citizens from the electoral process that it may choose." By restricting the vote to those with money to pay for it, Marshall said, Virginia was violating the Fourteenth Amendment's guarantee of "equal protection of the laws." Once more, the solicitor general's arguments prevailed. In a 6–3 decision, the Supreme Court struck down the Virginia poll tax. "Wealth, like race, creed, or color," said Justice Hugo Black, "is not germane to one's ability to participate intelligently in the electoral process."

During Marshall's tenure as solicitor general, the Supreme Court heard a number of cases dealing with the right to privacy, another subject close to Marshall's heart. The Fourth Amendment protects Americans from "unreasonable searches and seizures." Years earlier, in 1928, the Supreme Court had ruled that the prohibition against unreasonable searches applied to speech as well as the "persons, houses, papers, and effects" listed in the amendment. Evidence obtained by wiretapping had been banned in all courtooms since 1934. But Marshall, who held an even broader view of unreasonable searches, considered all electronic eavesdropping illegal.

In 1966, when the Supreme Court scheduled *Black v. United States*, a government case against a man accused of evading federal taxes, Marshall dropped a bombshell. The government's case, he told the Court, had been based on FBI wiretaps of telephone conversations between the defendant and his attorney. To Marshall's way of thinking, this procedure had resulted in an unfair trial. Instead of arguing for the United States, then, he asked the Court to send the case back to the district court, where the evidence obtained by the wiretap could be reevaluated. To the surprise of many legal observers, the Supreme Court granted Marshall's request, reversing the defendant's conviction until the evidence was reexamined.

Despite a staggering load of legal work, the apparently tireless Marshall found time to make frequent speeches at colleges and public meetings across the country. In a National Law Day speech in 1966, he lit into lawyers and "intellectuals" who criticized the Supreme Court's constantly shifting interpretation of the Constitution. Such criticism, he said, "reflects a profound element of misunderstanding [and] a refusal to . . . view the law, not as a set of abstract and socially unrelated commands . . . but as an effective instrument of social policy."

The Marshalls relax at home with their sons, Thurgood, Jr. (left), and John William, in the 1960s. A once-legendary poker player, Marshall told a reporter that since the arrival of the boys, his card playing had been reduced to games of War.

In another speech, this one delivered to the White House Conference on Civil Rights, Marshall outlined the long history of American blacks' battle for their rights. The Supreme Court's rulings on school segregation, "white primaries," and restrictive covenants, he said, had produced impressive improvements, but the time to relax had not arrived. "I advocate more laws and stronger laws," Marshall stated emphatically. "And the passage of such laws requires untiring efforts."

Arguing before the Supreme Court, writing briefs, holding conferences with his staff at the Justice Department, and making speeches required what Marshall once estimated as 23 hours a day. Nevertheless, the solicitor general found time to enjoy his home life. On weekends, the boys played touch football with their father on the lawn; during the week, they attended the Georgetown Day School. Cissy Marshall's many activities included planning and presiding over the family's frequent dinner parties, whose guests comprised some of the capital's most glittering personalities.

At home, Marshall liked to relax in the kitchen. When he was a boy, his maternal grandmother, Mary Eliza Williams, had taught him to cook. "I'm all with your parents in wanting you to be a professional man," she told him, "but I want to be sure you can always earn a dollar. You can pick up all that other stuff later, but I bet you never saw a jobless Negro cook." Marshall managed to "earn a dollar" outside the kitchen, but he enjoyed cooking for friends. Fans of his cuisine especially praised his she-crab soup, a Baltimore specialty, and his horseradish-laden concoctions. One longtime friend, singer Lena Horne, insisted that Marshall "cooks the best pig feet in the world."

Other Marshall spare-time pursuits included horse racing and listening to jazz and symphonic music. "I don't know all the titles and composers," he once confessed, "I just like it." And, despite his denials, Marshall was a confirmed addict of movie westerns, sometimes watching TV reruns of his old favorites for hours. As he once explained, he was "still waiting to see one showing where the Indians win."

In 1967, Marshall was comfortably settled in both public and private life. But changes lay ahead. The president of the United States had new plans for his solicitor general. ✺

8

SUPREME COURT JUSTICE

Cissy Marshall makes a last-minute adjustment to her husband's robe before his 1967 U.S. Supreme Court swearing-in ceremony. The 96th man to take the oath, Marshall became the first black justice in the Court's 178-year history.

ON THE SUNNY morning of June 13, 1967, Lyndon Johnson and Thurgood Marshall faced a battery of television cameras in the White House Rose Garden. The president had just named the solicitor general as his choice for the vacancy on the Supreme Court. "He deserves the appointment," said Johnson. "He is the best qualified by training and by very valuable service to the country." The president paused, then said forcefully, "I believe it is the right thing to do, the right time to do it, the right man and the right place. I believe he has already earned his place in history, but I think it will be greatly enhanced by his service on the Court."

Millions of people rejoiced at Johnson's words. Echoing the sentiments of many of his fellow citizens, Floyd B. McKissick, chairman of the Congress of Racial Equality (CORE), a prominent civil rights organization, said, "This has stirred pride in the breast of every black American."

Thurgood Marshall would be the first native of Maryland to serve on the Supreme Court since Roger Taney, chief justice from 1836 until 1864. Taney had presided over the celebrated case of Dred Scott, a Missouri slave who claimed the right to freedom after living in the free Wisconsin Territory for several years. His case reached the Supreme Court in 1856. Delivering the Court's ruling in 1857, Taney said that because Scott was a Negro, he was "property," not a citizen. Therefore, said Taney, Scott had no rights under the Constitution and no right to institute a

Marshall listens to a question posed by a member of the Senate Judiciary Committee in July 1967, during the hearings to confirm his nomination to the U.S. Supreme Court. He was sworn in as an associate justice three months later.

lawsuit. (The sympathetic son of Scott's former master later arranged to purchase the black man, whom he immediately emancipated.)

Now, little more than a century after that fateful decision, the great-grandson of a slave stood at the side of the president of the United States. A free American citizen, a distinguished attorney, and a powerful reformer, Thurgood Marshall was about to take his place on the Court where Roger Taney had ruled that blacks were property, not people. Slowly, painfully, but steadily, the nation was moving forward.

Johnson later talked to an interviewer about Marshall. "I figured he'd be a great example to younger kids," said the president. "All over America that day, Negro parents looked at their children a little differently, thousands of mothers looked across the breakfast table and said, 'Now, maybe this will happen to my child someday.' I bet from one coast to the other, there was a rash of new mothers naming their newborn sons Thurgood."

Johnson's announcement sparked an avalanche of comments, most of them positive, in the nation's press. New York City's leading black newspaper, the *Amsterdam News,* called the nomination "a milestone in American history." *Newsweek,* which said Marshall had "probably done as much to transform the life of his people as any Negro alive today, including Nobel laureate Martin Luther King," called him "the legal champion of the Negro revolution." Marshall's nomination, said the magazine, offered "fresh evidence that America may romanticize its radicals, but it more often rewards its reformers. And Marshall is a reformer in the best tradition of the rule of law."

In a letter to the president, Supreme Court Chief Justice Earl Warren said, "All of us know Thurgood, and will welcome him to the Court in the belief that he will make a real contribution." Not everyone, however, agreed: In some quarters, the spirit of Roger Taney lived on. This time, Marshall's confirmation hearings were even more hostile than those he had endured for the Second Circuit court.

Die-hard southern senators did their best to humiliate the nominee during the hearings. South Carolina's Strom Thurmond was the roughest. He confronted Marshall with a list of 60 complex questions about the post–Civil War Congress and its dealings with constitutional issues. Marshall, who had told friends he was determined to "keep a cool head" during the hearings, calmly admitted that he was unable to answer most of Thurmond's questions. Later, when North Carolina's Sam Ervin questioned Marshall's ability to exercise judicial restraint, Senator Joseph D. Tydings of Maryland sprang to the nominee's defense. Marshall's "performance in the last two days," said Tydings pointedly, "is a great testimony to his judicial restraint."

When the Judiciary Committee reported its findings to the full Senate, Thurmond announced that Marshall had failed to pass the simple test of history he had been given. It was "surprising," said Thurmond, that Marshall could not even name the congressional research committee members who had worked on the Fourteenth Amendment in 1868. At this point, Senator Edward Kennedy of Massachusetts interrupted Thurmond. Did the senator from South Carolina, he asked politely, "have that information at hand?" If so, said Kennedy, he would appreciate Thurmond's reading it into the record. Obviously unable to produce the names himself, the flustered Thurmond hastily concluded his remarks and sat down.

Despite the southerners' harassment, Marshall won full Senate approval by a vote of 69 to 11. He took the oath of office one month later, on October 2, 1967. Seated next to President Johnson, the proud

Marshall family—Cissy, Thurgood, Jr., and John William—watched Thurgood Marshall as he placed his hand on a Bible and swore to "administer justice without respect to persons, and do equal right to the poor and to the rich." After taking the oath, a beaming Associate Justice Marshall shook hands with his fellow justices and went to work, joining his colleagues as they admitted a group of lawyers to practice before the Court.

During Marshall's first term, the Supreme Court heard 110 cases. As a former solicitor general, he disqualified himself from participating in 57 of these cases because the government had an interest in them. Of the remaining cases, Marshall wrote 14 opinions, the most significant of which dealt with First Amendment rights and the rights of defendants.

One of these cases, *Interstate Circuit, Inc. v. City of Dallas*, centered on movie censorship and the right to freedom of expression. The city of Dallas had established a review board to decide what films were "likely to incite or encourage delinquency or sexual promiscuity on the part of young persons." Movies so identified were declared off limits to anyone under the age of 16. Challenged by a local film distributor, the legality of the Dallas film board came under Supreme Court review in early 1968. Marshall, speaking for the majority, ruled against Dallas. Because such terms as "sexual promiscuity" were too "vague" to apply with justice, he said, the Dallas film board's actions violated the First Amendment. In this opinion, Marshall emphasized the far-reaching effect of a Supreme Court ruling: "What Dallas may constitutionally do," he pointed out, "so may other cities and states."

Another free-speech case involved an Illinois schoolteacher who had criticized his board of education in a letter to the local newspaper. Fired for writing the letter, the teacher sued the school board; when an Illinois court upheld the board's decision,

The U.S. Supreme Court in 1967, with its newest member, Associate Justice Thurgood Marshall. Seated (left to right) are John M. Harlan, Hugo Black, Chief Justice Earl Warren, William O. Douglas, and William J. Brennan, Jr. In the back row (left to right) are Abe Fortas, Potter Stewart, Byron R. White, and Marshall.

the teacher took his case to the Supreme Court. Marshall, again speaking for the majority, said the ruling of the Illinois court implied that the teacher—or anyone else—could be forced to give up his First Amendment right of free speech in order to keep his job. Pointing out that such a premise had been rejected by the Court in numerous earlier decisions, Marshall decided for the teacher, reversing the lower court's decision.

When questioned about his political position, Marshall refused to identify himself with any philosophical or political camp. He did, however, offer clues. "I am not attached to any legal school of thought," he told one reporter. "But I am also not a conservative." As term followed term, his decisions proved that he was, as many court observers phrased it, "his own man." He remained skeptical, wary of change but willing to reconsider any traditions that appeared to be out of touch with the times. But his decisions made it clear that he would never retreat from his lifelong commitment to civil liberty.

"We're over the beginning on civil rights," Marshall had told a *New York Times* reporter in 1965. "There are, of course, plenty of important questions still hanging, involving such things as school picketing and street demonstrations. Now fundamentally, I believe I have the right to picket anybody's house with a sign that says, 'You're a bum.' But that doesn't give me the right to chain myself to the man's door. You just can't chain a doorway, whether it be to courts, homes, or stores."

Picketing was the subject of a 1968 case in which Marshall wrote the majority opinion. When a striking food employees' union picketed a store in a Pennsylvania shopping mall, the mall's owner sued, claiming that the strikers were trespassing on private property. Marshall disagreed. Although it was privately owned, he said, the mall was "clearly the functional equivalent" of a city business block and could not be sealed off from citizens exercising their constitutional rights of free expression and communication. "Peaceful picketing carried on in a location open generally to the public," Marshall concluded, "is protected by the First Amendment."

Some of Marshall's opinions—his ruling on a 1969 obscenity case, for example—created ripples of surprise among Court watchers. The 1969 case *Stanley v. Georgia* began with a police visit to the home of a Georgia man suspected of illegal bookmaking. The police, who had obtained a warrant permitting them to search for evidence of gambling, found something else instead: three reels of film they judged pornographic. Arrested and found guilty of possessing obscene material, the Georgia man appealed to the Supreme Court. The Court overturned the conviction, with Marshall asserting that "mere private possession" of the allegedly obscene films broke no law. His written opinion in the case left no doubt about his sentiments on the matter:

Whatever may be the justifications for other statutes regulating obscenity, we do not think they reach into the privacy of one's own home. If the First Amendment means anything, it means that a state has no business telling a man, sitting alone in his own house, what books he may read or what films he may watch. Our whole constitutional heritage rebels at the thought of giving government the power to control men's minds.

Such opinions strengthened Marshall's reputation for plain speaking. A blunt, direct questioner in court and a skillful debater at the justices' conferences, he seemed as likely to use intuitive common sense as to employ complex, legalistic reasoning. Behind the scenes, too, Marshall's straightforward style set him apart from the stereotype of a mannered and formal judge. Colleagues and clerks alike reported his attitude toward them as relaxed and amiable. Occasionally, however, fellow justices found his informality somewhat jarring.

Warren Burger, who became chief justice after Earl Warren's retirement in 1969, apparently needed a little time to get used to Associate Justice Marshall. In *The Brethren*, their 1979 book about the Supreme Court, authors Bob Woodward and Scott Armstrong quote Marshall's customary greeting to Burger in the Court halls: "What's shakin', Chiefy baby?" At first, the conservative Burger would simply look puzzled, mumble a few words in response, and walk rapidly on. As time passed, however, Burger grew to respect Marshall, and the two men established a cordial and respectful relationship.

Marshall also treated Court visitors to his own brand of humor. One day, he had just entered the justices' private elevator when a group of tourists boarded it by mistake. Assuming that the black man at the controls was the elevator operator, the visitors said, "First floor, please." Marshall responded with his best Uncle Tom imitation. "Yassah, yassah," he said, putting the elevator in motion and delivering the visitors to their destination. According to Woodward and Armstrong, "Marshall regularly recounted

Marshall joins Dr. George Allen (left), President Granville Sawyer, and law school dean Otis King (right) after a 1976 ceremony renaming the Texas Southern University School of Law. Of the approximately 100 men and women graduated each year by the Thurgood Marshall School of Law, about half are black, one-quarter Mexican American, and the remainder white.

Cecilia Marshall, daughter of the Marshalls' son John and a namesake of her grandmother, enjoys television with her grandfather in the early 1980s.

the story, noting the tourists' puzzlement and then confusion as they watched him walk off, and later realized who he was."

But Marshall's easygoing personal style was deceptive. Beneath the relaxed appearance and surface humor, he was as shrewd and tough-minded as ever. In the decades that followed his elevation to the high court, he remained unshakably committed to the defense of constitutional rights and the establishment of educational and legal equality for all races. In case after case, Marshall supported the positions of civil libertarians and equal rights advocates. In the beginning of his service as a justice, he often found himself voting with the Court's liberal majority.

But with the election of President Richard Nixon in 1968, the balance of the court began to change, becoming more conservative as the Republican president replaced retiring justices with members of his own choosing. Marshall now became one of the Court's most outspoken and emphatic dissenters. In the *Milliken v. Bradley* case, for example, he wrote a memorable dissent from the majority opinion.

Milliken, a Detroit case, reached the Supreme Court 20 years after the *Brown* decision. By the early 1970s, the South had desegregated many of its schools. The states of the North and the West, however, lagged behind in following the Court's 1954 ruling that separate but equal schools violated the Constitution. Like many other northern cities, Detroit had become a "bull's-eye"—an inner city populated largely by blacks, surrounded by rings of almost entirely white suburbs. As a result, the Michigan city's schools had reverted to a pattern of segregation. Instead of trying to integrate the schools, the Detroit board of education had made segregation even more pronounced by busing black students to black schools, even when white schools were closer, and by encouraging white students to transfer to white schools far from their own neighborhood.

When a group of black parents sued the state, the district court—later backed by the court of appeals—decided in their favor. Detroit, said the courts, must expand its school district to include many of the city's wealthy white suburbs. Students from all over this larger area, continued the courts, must be racially mixed, even if the move required massive busing. The United States Supreme Court, however, reversed the lower courts. Speaking for the now-conservative majority, Chief Justice Burger ruled that the integration plan placed an unfair burden on Detroit's suburban white population. Marshall, one of the four dissenting justices, expressed his opinion in passionate terms.

In Detroit, said Marshall, black children had been "intentionally confined to an expanding core of all-Negro schools immediately surrounded by a . . . band of all-white schools." He asserted that the issue concerned "the right of all of our children, whatever their race, to an equal start in life." America, he countinued, "will be ill-served by the Court's refusal to remedy separate and unequal education, for unless our children begin to learn together, there is little hope that our people will ever learn to live together." After "20 years of small, often difficult steps," Marshall concluded sadly, "the Court today takes a giant step backward."

Regents of the University of California v. Bakke inspired another strong Marshall dissent. The case began when the California institution's medical school rejected Alan Bakke, a highly qualified white applicant. The University of California practiced affirmative action, a program designed to correct the long-term imbalance of black and white students in the nation's colleges and corporations. Because the quota of minority students had filled all the medical school's openings, no slot remained for Bakke, despite his high scores on admissions tests. Claiming reverse discrimination, Bakke sued the university.

Cissy Marshall with her husband in 1988.

Bakke, which reached the Supreme Court in 1978, resulted in a mixed decision: Although race could be considered as one factor in admitting students, ruled the Court, rigid quotas for minorities were not permissible. Marshall thunderously disagreed. The Court, he said, had firmly obligated itself to eliminate racism in public life; now it was once again making a full-scale retreat from its own commitment.

As an associate justice of the Supreme Court, Marshall never hesitated to make his feelings known; outside the courtroom, however, he said little. Before he took his place on the high court, he had been a popular public speaker and the frequent subject of newspaper interviews and magazine profiles. After he ascended to the bench, he strictly limited his public statements, made personal appearances only on social occasions, and gave speeches only to legal gatherings. But in the fall of 1979, when Howard University installed a new law school dean, Marshall made an exception to his policy and addressed the students of his alma mater. His speech contained a mixture of wry humor, advice, and recollections about his mentor, Howard Law School dean Charles H. Houston.

"You know," Marshall said, "I used to be amazed by people who would say that 'the poorest Negro kid in the South is better off than a black kid in South Africa.' So what? We are not *in* South Africa. We are *here*." Warming to his subject, Marshall added, "I am also amazed by people who say, 'You ought to go around the country and show yourself to Negroes and give them inspiration.' For what? These Negro kids are not fools. They know when you tell them there is a possibility that someday they'll have a chance to be the O-N-L-Y Negro on the Supreme Court, that those odds aren't too good. . . . Well, all I am trying to tell you is there's a lot more to be done. . . . There are people who tell us today . . .

Thoroughly at home in the U.S. Supreme Court by 1979, Marshall heads for the Court Robing Room with colleague William Brennan. The Court's tilt to the political right in the 1970s distressed Marshall, but he remained firmly committed to his ideals: Other members of the Court might try to reverse civil rights progress, he thundered in 1989, "but I'm not going to do it."

'Take it easy, man. You made it. No more to worry about. Everything is easy.' Again I remind you of Charlie Houston's words: 'You have got to be better, boy. You better move better.' "

Concluding his speech in a ringing voice, Marshall recalled the day in 1963 when the African nation of Kenya celebrated its independence. "Hundreds of thousands of people," he said, "yelled in unison the watchword of that day and of this day— *Harambee!*—meaning 'Pull together!'" The entire student body rose to its feet, cheering and applauding the former Howard law student.

Anguished by what he saw as more than a decade of backsliding on civil liberties, Marshall spoke out again in a 1987 interview. Although Supreme Court justices almost never comment on political issues, Marshall could not resist answering a reporter who asked him to evaluate President Ronald Reagan's contributions to black America. Reagan, snapped the justice, "has done zero for civil rights."

In September 1989, after 22 years at the Supreme Court, Marshall made a few more political comments, this time before an audience of federal judges. Supreme Court decisions of recent years, he said, had displayed an increasingly restrictive approach to civil liberties. And such decisions, he insisted, "put at risk not only the civil rights of minorities but the civil rights of all citizens." The Court, he asserted, was now deliberately reversing 35 years of progress on civil rights. "We could sweep it under the rug and hide it," said the angry justice, "but I'm not going to do it." No one familiar with Thurgood Marshall's career could doubt his words.

On June 27, 1991, after more than two decades of distinguished service as an Associate Justice, Marshall retired from the court. Two years later, on January 24, 1993, he died of heart failure in Maryland. "Inscribed above the front entrance to the Supreme Court building are the words 'Equal justice under law,' " Chief Justice William H. Rehnquist said in his eulogy. "Surely no one individual did more to make these words a reality than Thurgood Marshall."

History will record Marshall as the first black American to sit on the Supreme Court. But perhaps an even more important achievement was his orchestration of the *Brown* case, which demolished the legal basis for segregation in America. When Marshall took over the NAACP Legal Defense Fund in

1938, racial discrimination was a fact of American life. Black children attended separate, inferior schools. They bathed at separate beaches, drank from separate water fountains, entered theaters from separate doors. When they grew up, society restricted them to jobs at the lowest end of the economic scale. In many parts of the nation, they were denied the right to vote, the right to a fair trial, the right to live where they wanted to live. Not even their lives were safe: In the first half of the 20th century, lynch mobs murdered thousands of black men and women.

In persuading the Supreme Court to rule school segregation unconstitutional, Marshall scored a tremendous victory. The decision by no means eradicated racial prejudice or even immediately eliminated school segregation. In some areas of American life, progress was slow and painful. But *Brown* changed the social climate of the nation, paving the way for laws that prohibited discrimination in housing, employment, public facilities, and the armed services. The decision marked the place in history when the government of the United States stopped sanctioning and supporting racial inequality.

One of the most successful constitutional lawyers of the 20th century, Marshall has also served as a symbol of hope and courage to citizens of all races. Historians agree that, in the long run, no government can succeed or endure without extending justice to all its citizens. By employing legal and peaceful means to advance blacks both politically and socially, Marshall has not only made an immense contribution to all Americans but to the foundation of American justice itself. ◆

CHRONOLOGY

1908   Born Thoroughgood Marshall on July 2 in Baltimore, Maryland

1929   Marries Vivian Burey

1930   Graduates with honors from Lincoln University

1933   Receives law degree from Howard University; begins private practice in Baltimore

1934   Begins to work for Baltimore branch of the National Association for the Advancement of Colored People (NAACP)

1935   With Charles Houston, wins first major civil rights case, *Murray v. Pearson*

1936   Becomes assistant special counsel for NAACP in New York

1940   Appointed director-counsel for NAACP Legal Defense and Educational Fund; with *Chambers v. Florida*, wins first of 27 Supreme Court victories

1944   Successfully argues *Smith v. Allwright*, overthrowing the South's "white primary"; suffers the first of four Supreme Court defeats with *Lyons v. Oklahoma*

1946   Receives Spingarn Medal from NAACP

1948   Wins *Shelley v. Kraemer*, in which Supreme Court strikes down legality of racially restrictive covenants

1950   Wins Supreme Court victories in two graduate-school integration cases, *Sweatt v. Painter* and *McLaurin v. Oklahoma State Regents*

1951   Visits South Korea to investigate charges of racism in U.S. armed forces

1954   Wins *Brown v. Board of Education of Topeka*, landmark case that demolishes legal basis for segregation in America

1955   Following death of first wife, marries Cecilia Suyat

1961   Defends civil rights demonstrators, winning Supreme Court victory in *Garner v. Louisiana*; nominated to Second Circuit Court of Appeals by President John F. Kennedy

1961–65   As circuit judge, makes 98 rulings, all of them later upheld by Supreme Court

1965   Appointed U.S. solicitor general by President Lyndon Johnson; wins 14 of the 19 cases he argues for the government between 1965 and 1967

1967   Becomes first black American elevated to U.S. Supreme Court; as associate justice, continues to support constitutional rights and educational and legal equality for all races

1991   Announces his retirement on June 27

1993   Dies of heart failure on January 24 at Bethesda Naval Medical Center, Maryland

FURTHER READING

Abraham, Henry J. *Justices and Presidents: A Political History of Appointments to the Supreme Court.* New York: Oxford University Press, 1974.

Berman, Daniel M. *It Is So Ordered: The Supreme Court Rules on School Segregation.* New York: Norton, 1966.

Bland, Randall W. *Private Pressure on Public Law: The Legal Career of Justice Thurgood Marshall.* New York: Associated Faculty Press, 1973.

Clayton, James E. *The Making of Justice: The Supreme Court in Action.* New York: Dutton, 1964.

Fenderson, Lewis H. *Thurgood Marshall: Fighter for Justice.* New York: McGraw-Hill/Rutledge, 1969.

Friedman, Leon, and Fred L. Israel. *The Justices of the United States Supreme Court, 1789–1969: Their Lives and Major Opinions.* 5 vols. New York: Chelsea House, 1980.

Kluger, Richard. *Simple Justice.* New York: Knopf, 1976.

Manchester, William. *The Glory and the Dream: A Narrative History of America, 1932–1972.* Boston: Little, Brown, 1974.

Miller, Loren. *The Petitioners: The Story of the Supreme Court of the United States and the Negro.* Cleveland: World Publishing, 1966.

Schwartz, Bernard, ed. *Statutory History of the United States: Civil Rights, Part I.* New York: Chelsea House, 1970.

Schwartz, Bernard, with Stephan Lesher. *Inside the Warren Court.* Garden City, NY: Doubleday, 1983.

William, Juan. *Eyes on the Prize: America's Civil Rights Years, 1954–1965.* New York: Viking-Penguin, 1987.

Woodward, Bob, and Scott Armstrong. *The Brethren.* New York: Avon Books, 1981.

INDEX

PICTURE CREDITS